Baba Bulleh Shah

A selection of his Punjabi Poetry

A new translation by

Dr. Wasim Ahmed

Dedicated to the loving memory of my dearest sister, Saroj.

Contents

Acknowledgements. i

Introduction. iii

The life and times of Baba Bulleh Shah. v

Part 1 – Poems in English, Gurmukhi & Shahmukhi 1

1. If God could be found (Jai Rab Milda). 2

2. Essence (Muqeed). 4

3. Ocean of love (Ishq Sammundar). 6

4. Fragile heart (Naazuk Dil). 8

5. Rising Suns (Churrdhay suraj). 10

6. Sectarianism (Firka-bundhi). 12

7. In a single point (Ik nuktay wich). 14

8. The One sitting at home (Ghur bettha). 18

9. Bullehya! What I know who I am (Bullehya! Ki jannan main kon). 20

10. Dogs are higher than you! (Kuttay tehthoon uttay!) 24

11. Inside and out (Undher, baaher). 26

12. Neither am I Hindu, nor Muslim (Hindu nah, naahin Mussalman). 28

13. Going to Mecca (Mukkay gaiyan). 30

14. It is just You! (Tuhiyoon ain!) 32

15. Raze the temple (Mandir dha dai). 34

16. Enough of your learning, o friend! (Ilmoon bus kurrin o yaar!) 36

17. Some ask! (Koi puccho!) 44

18. What repentance? (Kaissi toba?) 46

19. Accomplished Teacher (Kamil Murshid). 50

20. Just chant Alif (Ik Alif purrho!) 52

21. Let it be (Bus kar ji). 56

22. The nature of God and man (Rab tai bundhay di zaat). 60

23. White or black (Gori ya kaali). 62

24. Wake up! (Utth jaag!) 64

25. Take out this timekeeper! (Ghurryali daiwo nikaal ni!) 68

26. Difficult! (Okha!) 72

27. Birds. (Punchi). 74

28. Faith in One God (Tawheed). 76

29. I am without confines! (Main bay-kaidh!) 78

30. Ranjha, Ranjha. (Ranjha, Ranjha). 80

31. Haji folk (Haji lok). 84

32. Such perverse times have come (Ultay hor zummanay ayai). 88

33. Now, who are You hiding Yourself from? (Hunh kis thin aap chuppai dha?) 92

34. They Came to persuade Bulleh (Bulleh noon sumjhawan ayiyan). 96

35. Show me your abode (Apna dhus tikaana). 100

36. True love (Ishq). 104

37. Ego (Nafs). 106

38. Friend (Yaar). 108

39. This true Love (Ais Ishq). 110

40. Ram, Raheem and Maula (Ram, Raheem tai Maula). 112

Part 2 – Transliteration 117

1. Jai Rab Milda. 118

2. Muqeed. 119

3. Ishq sammundar. 120

4. Naazuk dil. 121

5. Churrdhay suraj. 122

6. Firka-bundhi. 123

7. Ik nuktay wich. 124

8. Ghur bettha. 125

9. Bullehya! ki jannan main kon. 126

10. Kuttay tehthoon uttay! 127

11. Undher, baaher. 128

12. Hindu nah, naahin Mussalman. 129

13. Mukkay gaiyan. 130

14. Tuhiyoon ain! 131

15. Mandir dha dai. 132

16. Ilmoon bus kurrin o yaar! 133

17. Koi Puccho! 135

18. Kaissi toba? 136

19. Kamil Murshid. 137

20. Ik Alif purrho! 138

21. Bus kar ji. 139

22. Rab tai bundhay di zaat. 140

23. Gori ya kaali. 141

24. Utth jaag! 142

25. Ghurryali daiwo nikaal ni! 143

26. Okha! 144

27. Punchi. 145

28. Tawheed. 146

29. Main bay-kaidh! 147

30. Ranjha, Ranjha. 148

31. Haji lok. 149

32. Ultay hor zummanay ayai. 150

33. Hunh kis thin aap chuppai dha? 151

34. Bulleh noon sumjhawan ayiyan. 152

35. Apna dhus tikaana. 153

36. Ishq. 154

37. Nafs. 155

38. Yaar. 156

39. Ais Ishq. 157

40. Ram, Raheem tai Maula. 158

Acknowledgements.

First and foremost, my sincere gratitude goes to Mrs. Sheena Whiteley, who not only taught me how to speak English but also taught me that nothing is impossible if one tries hard enough.

I cannot thank enough, Mr. Ian Doyle, for his technical support, helpful suggestions, and proof-reading of this book.

My grateful thanks go to Dr. Tasneem Sulaiman who helped enormously in finding meanings of obscure and forgotten Punjabi words.

I would like to thank Ranveer Singh, of Khalis House Publishing, who saw the value of the work of Baba Bulleh Shah, and like me, wishes to preserve such Punjabi cultural heritage for future generations. I would also like to thank Ranveer for providing the transliteration of the Shahmukhi into Gurmukhi script in the hope that the book will be able to reach a wider audience.

Introduction.

When asked to name a famous Sufi poet philosopher, most people would think of the great Jalal ul Din Rumi (1207 - 1273) as his writings have had a profound effect on people's spiritual thinking over many centuries. Rumi's poetry still consistently tops poetry sales in the United States. One of the reasons why Rumi is so well known and admired around the world is because his work has been available in translation now for over two hundred years. Through translation, not only has his work been brought to the attention of a new and wider audience but it has also been preserved for ever.

Originating from Jammu and Kashmir and being familiar with the rich traditions of the great Sufi poets from the Punjab, Sindh and Balochistan, I have often wondered why the work of these great Sufi saints has not been disseminated more widely.

The tradition of Sufi poetry in this region began with Baba Farid Ganjshakar (1173-1265), a contemporary of Rumi. He was born in Kothewal, near Multan in modern day Pakistan. Instead of writing in Farsi, which was the academic language at the time, Baba Farid chose to write in his native Punjabi and raised this great regional language to new heights. Written Punjabi literature began with Baba Farid, and it has influenced thinkers and philosophers ever since. Some of his work is included in the Guru Granth Sahib, and he is rightly known as the father of Punjabi literature.

The Punjabi language can be written in two forms, the Gurmukhi script formalised by Guru Angad Dev ji and the Shahmukhi script written using the Arabic alphabet. These forms used by Baba Farid, have continued to be used by the great poets who came after him. The Punjabi language has naturally evolved over time and unfortunately the classic forms of Punjabi are now becoming less well understood. Although the poetry of the great Sufi Saints is still widely popular and frequently recited and quoted in public, its meaning is not always fully understood. Added to this is the fact that population shifts from the Punjabi-speaking regions of India and Pakistan to the western world has resulted in a generation whose first language is English rather than Punjabi. This generation has no means of linking with the rich literary heritage of their ancestors as they have become unfamiliar with their mother tongue.

Currently there is a great thirst for knowledge of their history and culture by the descendents of migrants from the Punjabi-speaking regions of northen India and Pakistan, and this is only just being recognised. Losing one's native language is the first step to losing one's identity and this can lead to feelings of alienation and rejection. More and more people are recognising that our history and literature must be preserved and made more accessible for future generations or it will be lost forever.

We can see from the example of Rumi's work that one way of preserving and permeating works of literature is by translating them into English. I have chosen to do this for one of the greatest Sufi poets of the Punjab, Baba Bulleh Shah, whose work is extremely popular throughout the Punjabi-speaking world and is still a favourite choice for setting to popular music and used in main-stream cinema.

Baba Bulleh Shah, as we will see, was a great Sufi Saint who taught that God resides within each one of us, and that we need to search and make a home for Him within our own hearts before we start looking for Him elsewhere. He was born at a time of great upheaval and strife in the Punjab and taught a message of love, equality, peace, and harmony between people of all Faiths.

The internet and social media are awash with sites sharing the poetry of Baba Bulleh Shah with comments often pleading for translation of his words. When a translation is given, it is often of an inadequate standard as it may be just literal without considering the subject matter or context. Unusual or difficult words may be misinterpreted or even changed altogether.

Translation of this type of poetry can be very challenging as the Punjabi language is so rich and beautiful and often one word may have many meanings. Added to this is the difficulty of the mystical element where the descriptive language is being used as a metaphor for complex spiritual concepts. The context and the tense are extremely important in order to convey the true meaning of the Verse, and this can be difficult to do, while preserving the mood of the stanza.

Having said all this, I am adding my interpretation to the mix! I have tried extremely hard to translate accurately and to avoid making mistakes but as will become obvious, in verses with multiple meanings, this will be difficult to avoid. I beg the reader to forgive any failings I might display.

The life and times of Baba Bulleh Shah.

The exact date of Bulleh Shah's birth is not known but it is thought to be in the year 1680 that Sayyid Sakhi Shah Mohammed Darwaish and his wife Fatima Bibi were blessed with a healthy baby boy. The happy parents named him Abdullah Shah. He is known to have had at least one older and two younger sisters but must also have had brothers as he mentions 'sisters -in-law' in his poetry later.

The place of his birth was a small village called Uch Gillanian in the Punjab province of the then Mughal Empire, now in modern day Pakistan. Sakhi Shah Mohammed Darwaish was employed as the Imam at the village mosque; a modest job that involved duties of leading the five daily Muslim prayers, giving the weekly Friday Sermon, and teaching the village children to read the Quran. It was a humble position and would have barely provided enough for the family to survive. Payment was in kind at harvest time when people from the village presented him with flour, oil, pulses, and other produce which kept the family going until the following harvest. Income would have been supplemented by performing marriage ceremonies, funerals and attending other religious functions during the year when the hosts would hopefully make donations of clothes or food.

It is believed that Abdullah Shah's ancestors had originated from Halb (Aleppo) in Syria. The first of these ancestors to migrate to Uch was Shaikh Bandagi Mohammed Ghaus who arrived in the Punjab almost two hundred years before Abdullah Shah was born. Although poverty stricken, they had one asset in that they were 'Sayyids', or directly descended from the family of the holy Prophet Mohammed, peace be upon him. As such they were held in high regard and would have been treated with respect. But being a Sayyid was a double-edged sword as it demanded exemplary behaviour and avoidance of menial and most manual jobs. The family would have had to maintain their dignity and would have refrained from asking for help, even in difficult circumstances.

Abdullah Shah's father inevitably had to move from village to village in search of better prospects. The family initially moved to Malakwal when he was six months old and his father then took up a position as Imam at the village mosque in Pandoke, south of Lahore, when he was aged six. Initial education would have been provided with the rest of the village children by his father and he was then sent for higher studies to a well-respected scholar, Hafiz Ghulam Murtaza, who had set up a college in the city of Kasur, fifty miles south of Pandoke, Punjab.

As a child, Abdullah Shah, was thought to be rather aloof and headstrong and prone to day-dreaming. He was known to the villagers by his nickname Bulla, short for Abdullah but this may also have been a play on the word 'Bhulla' meaning lost or forgotten. The nickname stuck and as he grew older it was adapted to a more respectful Bulleh Shah. Subsequently he has become renowned as Baba Bulleh Shah, acquiring the honorific 'Baba' meaning father or revered person.

Being born the son of the village Imam, Bulleh Shah would have been grounded in religious education and practice from an early age. Higher education would have taught him everything about Islamic thought, jurisprudence, the Quran and the Sunnat, and Bulleh Shah strictly followed the tenets of the Islamic Faith. He was fluent in Sanskrit, Arabic, Farsi (Persian) and Punjabi and had a deep knowledge of Divinity and Theology of all the major religions around him.

Despite this, he felt a craving for more answers as to what was the purpose of life. He strongly believed that there was a One True Universal God but could not make sense of why He was so hidden. In order to find God and experience His light, Bulleh Shah decided that he needed to find an accomplished Teacher or Guide (Murshid or Guru) who might be able to help him in his quest.

Bulleh Shah was familiar with the reputation of just such a Guide, Baba Shah Innayat Qadiri Shatari (1643-1728). He was born and brought up in Kasur, Punjab, now in modern day Pakistan. Kasur at that time, however, was ruled over by strict Sunni Afghan lords as part of the Mughal Empire, and as Shah Innayat's reputation spread, they became irritated of his influence and started looking for ways to criticise his religious practices and eventually encouraged him to leave the city. Shah Innayat then took up residence in the much more liberal, cosmopolitan city of Lahore, known as the Pearl of the Punjab. This is where Bulleh Shah came to find and test him.

Islam does not subscribe to a caste system and all believers are equal under God. In reality, however, in the South Asian Subcontinent (modern-day India and Pakistan) at this time, Muslim society was divided according to people's trades and people tended to stay within these trades in terms of marriage and their social dealings. Some trades were considered higher and more important than others and people tended to resist associating or marrying into families of a lower standing than their own.

No trade or caste, however, can trump being a Sayyid, even if from a poor background. Here again the double-edged sword of belonging to the Noble Family created difficulties for Bulleh Shah as the Guide he was searching for belonged to the Arrain clan who were of farming background and although of a decent enough trade, still well below the standing of a Sayyid.

Thoughts along this line did occur to Bulleh Shah as to whether it was right to take on a Teacher who was of a lower social rank than himself, but he rejected them as he was against any divisions on the basis of race, colour or creed. What mattered to him the most was the character of the person and the light that he carried within him. The same thoughts obviously crossed Shah Innayat's mind also when he met Bulleh Shah, and he confronted him about it but Bulleh Shah put his mind at rest in this matter.

The first meeting of Teacher and pupil must have been pivotal as it has generated so many myths and legends with many versions of how the two men met. It is not in the scope of this book to go into all of them here but needless to say the recognition of greatness in the other was instant on both parts.

One realistic sounding narrative describes how Bulleh Shah was wondering around Lahore looking for Shah Innayat but had no idea of what he looked like. One day he headed for the shade of the Shalimar gardens in the city and saw a gardener tending to the borders. Bulleh Shah started talking to him about his search for God and the purpose of life, finally asking him;

"Eh Rab ki kurdha?", or what does God do?

To this, the gardener stood up and pointing with his trowel replied;

"O Bullehya! Rab ehdroon putdha ai tay odhur landha ai!"

O Bullehya! God reaps here and sows there!

This simple reply opened up Bulleh Shah's eyes and he knew that he was in the presence of Shah Innayat. He immediately knelt in front of him and taking his hand in his own, offered his oath of allegiance which Shah Innayat accepted. Thus, Bulleh Shah became the pupil of Shah Innayat and eventually succeeded him as the head of his religious Order on his death.

Although Bulleh Shah and Shah Innayat had set aside differences in terms of their 'castes' the arrangement was far from accepted by the wider families. Shah Innayat's wider family members seem to have suffered from an inferiority complex in the presence of Bulleh Shah, and Bulleh shah's family felt that he had brought shame on his family by taking on a Teacher below his own standing.

In his poem "Bulleh noon sumjahawan ayiyan" (see poem 34) Bulleh shah describes his sisters and sisters-in-law coming to harangue him about what he had done to bring shame on his Sayyid background by taking on an Arrain Teacher and to desist from his folly, but he rejected their arguments saying that the true caste of a person was what was inside their heart.

They also tried to persuade Bulleh Shah to get married, but he rejected the idea as he was on a quest to find God and to devote his life to Him (the Beloved) alone. This he would not be able to do if he had a wife and children to care for (the likely reason his family wanted him to marry so he could be distracted from his Sufi path). Thus, Bulleh Shah devoted himself, body and soul to God and remained celibate his entire life.

Holy men and saints from the South Asian subcontinent are often ascribed elaborate myths and stories of miraculous powers by their followers. This is natural where men of such high integrity are born that others begin to see a powerful, positive, almost supernatural energy working through them. It is no different for Bulleh Shah who was said to have started showing miraculous powers at an early age and people attend his shrine to this day, asking for his help to intercede on their behalf.

Bulleh Shah lived at a very turbulent time in the history of the Punjab. The sixth Mughal Emperor, Aurangzeb Alamgir (1618 - 1707) had taken the Peacock throne in 1658 after his father Emperor Shah Jahan became ill and proclaimed a rival son, Dara Shikoh as his heir. Aurangzeb saw this as a betrayal and took up arms against his brother, defeated and killed him in battle and took the Crown from him. Later when Shah Jahan recovered from his illness, Aurangzeb had him declared unfit to be Emperor and punished him for his betrayal by imprisoning him in the Agra Fort opposite the Taj Mahal which he had had built in memory of his wife Mumtaz.

Aurangzeb was the last of the Great Mughal rulers and unlike some of his predecessors, was a strict Muslim. He had the "Fatwa Alamgiri" declared changing Mughal Hindustan into an Islamic State and implemented Muslim Sharia Law on the country. A stricter implementation of Islamic Laws led to the banning of music and dance for the Muslims. Sufis praise God by singing praises to Him in the form of Qawwali and when a state of ecstasy overcomes them, they dance and try to achieve oneness with the Beloved. Such events would have been the norm at Bulleh Shah's base and soon Fatwas, religious edicts, started to be issued by religious authorities against him. Bulleh Shah, however, was not cowed by these impositions and continued despite increasingly shrill criticisms.

Aurangzeb was the last effective Mughal Ruler and after his death, the Empire started to slowly decline. As the Centre became weak, internal, and external forces started to take advantage. Law and order began to break down and widespread hunger and starvation took hold. One of the reasons for this was that the Mughal Treasury had been comprehensively looted by multiple incursions into Hindustan by the Afghan Durrani Emperor, Ahmed Shah Abdali (1722 - 1773) who invaded no less than eight times between 1748 and 1767, each time carting away as much treasure as possible. This became such a regular pattern that people began to share a proverb:

"Khadha, peeta, laahi dha, baaki Ahmed Shaahi dha!"

What you eat, drink and wear is yours, the rest belongs to Ahmed Shah!

Baba Bulleh Shah was a true humanist and the plight of the people of Punjab and the destruction of his homeland was extremely upsetting for him. He frequently writes about how food hoarders were causing starvation and how innocent people were being punished but the wicked set free. At this time, he is known to have instigated various construction works at his camp to provide a means of labour so people could earn some money to pay for food for their families.

The Punjab of Bulleh Shah's time was a vast and rich province of the Mughal Empire and was made up of a pleural society of Hindus and Muslims but where a new cultural force was slowly emerging. Sikhs, disciples of Baba Guru Nanak Dev Ji (1469 - 1539) had been gaining in numbers throughout the Punjab and were being seen as a threat to the power of the Mughal empire. Their leaders, Gurus, had been bitterly hunted and killed and a form of guerrilla warfare was being waged by their followers. Aurangzeb wanted to crush Sikh power once and for all in the Punjab and five years before Bulleh Shah was born, the ninth Guru of the Sikhs, Guru Tegh Bahadur Singh (1621 - 1675) was captured and beheaded in Delhi.

After him, his son, the tenth and last Guru, Guru Gobind Singh, started to organise the Sikhs into an organised, warrior community in the early 1700s. This was called the Khalsa movement, and Bulleh Shah would have witnessed this change at first hand. Guru Gobind Singh's sons were also killed by Mughal forces. In 1708 Guru Gobind Singh declared the Granth Sahib as the final living Guru for Sikhs to follow.

Baba Bulleh Shah was against any persecution on the basis of race, religion, colour, caste or gender. There was nothing as important to him as human life, all else being secondary, and he saw the presence of God in everyone. Religious strife caused suffering for all, and he did not believe in the loss of a single life on the basis of someone's religious beliefs. On many occasions he is known to have personally intervened to curtail violence between Muslims and Sikhs and counselled both sides not to spill innocent blood. This, however, made some people, particularly in the Muslim religious hierarchy, suspicious of his loyalties. The Muslim clergy were particularly incensed when in a poem, Bulleh Shah called the ninth Sikh Guru, Guru Tegh Bahadur Singh, a Ghazi, a term reserved for victorious Muslim holy warriors.

Bulleh Shah was a fearless man who stood up for his beliefs, whatever the consequences. He abhorred hypocrisy and exposed it at every level of society but especially in the religious hierarchy. He thus made many enemies within the Muslim religious elite who tried to bring him in line by having Fatwas or religious edicts, issued against him to desist, but these failed to cower him.

Born a Sayyid, Bulleh Shah, sought out the lowliest and poorest around him, and there is a particular legend that sets him apart from all other Sufi Saints. This describes how during a period of estrangement from his Guide, possibly caused by relatives of Shah Inaayat reporting to him that Baba Bulleh Shah had not shown them enough courtesy during a visit on account of his ego of being a Sayyid, Bulleh Shah left his base and set up camp near the red-light, courtesan district outside town. Here he observed how the courtesans beautified and dressed themselves to please their clients. These women were regarded as the lowest of society and Bulleh Shah lived amongst them, learned to dance and dress like them in order to completely destroy his ego of being a Sayyid. After many years, living like this, so the legend goes, he went with the troupe, veiled and dressed as a woman, and danced in front of his Teacher at his camp. When he revealed himself at the end, Shah Inayat told him that he knew it was him all along. Thus, Bulleh Shah proved to his Guide that he had well and truely conquered his ego and to prove this he would even dance as a common courtesan. Hence the two great Sufis were reconciled. Apart from his poetry, the legend of this dance has become one of Bulleh Shah's lasting legacies.

Baba Bulleh Shah rejected all notions of caste and creed and wished for all Faiths to live in peace and harmony. He was a close observer and lover of nature and a conservationist who encouraged people to plant trees and engage in deeds to generally benefit the community. Nothing made him happier than free food, Langar, being provided at his camp where Fakirs and general public alike could come and eat for free.

 Bulleh Shah taught compassion and good treatment of animals and was a lifelong vegetarian by choice.

Baba Bulleh Shah died peacefully in 1757 at the age of 77 years. He was refused burial at the communal Muslim cemetary due to objections by the religious elite he had criticized all his life and was buried at a separate place nearby in Kasur where a beautiful shrine has since been built and devotees attend constantly. Every year, to mark his death, a huge festival, Urs, is held at the shrine where people of all faiths attend from all over the world. The poetry of Baba Bulleh Shah is performed at these times in the traditional Qawwali style and devotees sing and dance as they did during his lifetime.

The legacy Baba Bulleh Shah has left is far-reaching and for many people his wisdom and poetry is as relevant today as it was 300 years ago.

Artistic impression of Baba Bulleh Shah

Part 1 – Poems in English, Gurmukhi & Shahmukhi

1. If God could be found (Jai Rab Milda).

If God could be found by bathing and washing,

Then He would have been found by frogs and fish!

If God could be found in jungles and plains,

Then He would have been found by cows and buffalos!

If God could be found in temples and mosques,

Then He would have been found by the frail and emaciated!

O Bullehya, God is found by those,

Whose intentions are true!

ਜੇ ਰੱਬ ਮਿਲਦਾ।

ਜੇ ਰੱਬ ਮਿਲਦਾ ਨ੍ਹਾਤਿਆਂ ਧੋਤਿਆਂ
ਤੇ ਓ ਮਿਲਦਾ ਡੱਡੂਆਂ ਮੱਛੀਆਂ ਨੂੰ

ਜੇ ਰੱਬ ਮਿਲਦਾ ਜੰਗਲ ਬੇਲਿਆਂ
ਤੇ ਓ ਮਿਲਦਾ ਗਾਈਆਂ ਬੱਛੀਆਂ ਨੂੰ

ਜੇ ਰੱਬ ਮਿਲਦਾ ਮੰਦਿਰ ਮਸੀਤੀਂ
ਤੇ ਓ ਮਿਲਦਾ ਛੁਮ ਛੱਣਿਕਿਆਂ ਨੂੰ

ਵੇ ਬੁੱਲ੍ਹਿਆ, ਰੱਬ ਓਹਨਾਂ ਨੂੰ ਮਿਲਦਾ
ਜਿੰਨਾ ਦੀਆਂ ਨੀਤਾਂ ਹੋਵਣ ਸੁੱਚੀਆਂ

١.   جے رب ملدا۔

جے رب ملدا نہاتیاں تھوتیاں،
تے او ملدا ڈڈھوواں مچھیاں نوں،

جے رب ملدا جنگل بیلیاں،
تے او ملدا گانیاں بچھیاں نوں ،

جے رب ملدا مندر مسیتی ،
تے او ملدا چھم چھڑڑیکیاں نوں،

وے بلھیا، رب اؤہناں نوں ملدا،
جنناں دیاں نیتاں ہوون سچیاں!

3

2. Essence (Muqeed).

If I search for You within me,

Then I know You are my essence,

If I search for You externally,

Then who pervades within me?

You are everything, You are within everyone,

I recognise You as the Holiest,

I am also You, You are also me,

Then who is this wretched Bullah?

ਮੁਕੀਦ

ਜੇ ਮੈਂ ਤੈਨੂੰ ਅੰਦਰ ਢੂੰਢਾਂ,
ਤੇ ਫਿਰ ਮੁਕੀਦ ਮੈਂ ਜਾਨਾਂ
ਜੇ ਮੈਂ ਤੈਨੂੰ ਬਾਹਰ ਢੂੰਢਾਂ
ਤੇ ਮੇਰੇ ਅੰਦਰ ਕੌਣ ਸਮਾਨਾ?

ਸਭ ਕੁੱਝ ਤੂੰ ਏਂ, ਸਭ ਵਿੱਚ ਤੂੰ ਏਂ,
ਸਭ ਤੋਂ ਪਾਕ ਪੇਚਾਨਾਂ
ਮੈਂ ਵੀ ਤੂੰ ਏਂ, ਤੂੰ ਵੀ ਮੈਂ ਹਾਂ,
ਵਤ ਬੁੱਲ੍ਹਾ ਕੌਣ ਨਿਮਾਨਾ?

۲.   مقید

جے میں تینوں اندر ڈھونڈاں،
تے پھیر مقید میں جاناں،
جے میں تینوں باہر ڈھونڈاں،
تے میرے اندر کون سمانا ؟

سب کجھ توں ایں، سب وچ توں ایں،
سب توں پاک پیچاناں،
میں وی توں ایں، توں وی میں ہاں،
وت بلھا کون نمانا ؟

3. Ocean of love (Ishq Sammundar).

Living surreptitiously, then what is to be dead?

What can you become like this, and what can you accomplish?

Since we ultimately must jump into the Ocean of love,

Then what is drowning, and what is it to swim?

ਇਸ਼ਕ ਸਮੁੰਦਰ।

ਲੁਕ ਲੁਕ ਜੀਣਾ ਤੇ ਮਰਨਾ ਕੀ?

ਇੰਜ ਹੋਣਾ ਕੀ, ਤੇ ਕਰਨਾ ਕੀ?

ਜਦ ਇਸ਼ਕ ਸਮੁੰਦਰੇ ਕੁਦ ਜਾਣਾ,

ਫੇਰ ਡੁੱਬਣਾ ਕੀ, ਤੇ ਤਰਨਾ ਕੀ?

٣. عشق سمندر .

لک لک جینا، تے مرنا کی؟

انج ہونا کی، تے کرنا کی؟

جد عشق سمندرے کد جاننڑھ ،

پھیر ڈبنا کی، تے ترنا کی؟

4. Fragile heart (Naazuk Dil).

We are people of a fragile heart,

Don't keep wounding our heart, my friend,

Don't keep making false promises, and

Don't keep taking false vows!

How many times have I said to you,

Don't keep testing me moment by moment!

I will die in remembrance of you,

Don't make me remember you so much!

ਨਾਜ਼ੁਕ ਦਿਲ

ਅਸੀ ਨਾਜ਼ੁਕ ਦਿਲ ਦੇ ਬੰਦੇ ਹਾਂ,

ਸਾਡਾ ਦਿਲ ਨਾ ਯਾਰ ਦੁਖਾਇਆ ਕਰ,

ਨਾ ਝੂਠੇ ਵਾਅਦੇ ਕਰਿਆ ਕਰ,

ਨਾ ਝੂਠੀਆਂ ਕਸਮਾਂ ਚਾਇਆ (ਖਾਇਆ)

ਕਰ

ਤੈਨੂੰ ਕਿੰਨੀ ਵਾਰੀ ਮੈ ਆਖਿਆ ਏ,

ਮੈਨੂੰ ਵਲ ਵਲ ਨਾ ਅਜ਼ਮਾਇਆ ਕਰ!

ਤੇਰੀ ਯਾਦ ਦੇ ਵਿੱਚ ਮਰ ਜਾਸਾਂ,

ਮੈਨੂੰ ਐਨਾ ਯਾਦ ਨਾ ਆਇਆ ਕਰ!

٤.   نازک دل .

اسی نازک دل دے بندے ہاں،

ساڈا دل نہ یار دکھایا کر،

نہ چھوٹھے وعدے کریا کر،

نہ چھوٹھیاں قسماں چایا کر

تینوں کنی واری میں آکھیا اے،

مینوں ول ول نہ ازمایا کر!

تیری یاد دے وچ میں مرجاساں،

مینوں اینا یاد نہ آیا کر!

5.   Rising Suns (Churrdhay suraj).

Rising suns, we have seen setting,

Doused lamps, we have seen ignited.

No one puts a value on the diamond,

Though fake coins traded, we have seen!

Those who have no one in this world,

Even those sons, we have seen prosper.

With His grace, o man,

People walking on water, we have seen!

People moan, lentils are not softening,

Melting stones, we have seen!

Those who failed to value the Beloved, Bullehya,

Rubbing their empty hands, we have seen!

ਚੜ੍ਹਦੇ ਸੂਰਜ।

ਚੜ੍ਹਦੇ ਸੂਰਜ ਢਲਦੇ ਵੇਖੇ,
ਬੁੱਝੇ ਦੀਵੇ ਬਲਦੇ ਵੇਖੇ,
ਹੀਰੇ ਦਾ ਕੋਈ ਮੁੱਲ ਨਾ ਤਾਰੇ,
ਖੋਟੇ ਸਿੱਕੇ ਚੱਲਦੇ ਵੇਖੇ।

ਜਿੰਨ੍ਹਾਂ ਦਾ ਨਾ ਜੱਗ ਤੇ ਕੋਈ,
ਓ ਵੀ ਪੁੱਤਰ ਪਲਦੇ ਵੇਖੇ
ਓਹਦੀ ਰਹਿਮਤ ਨਾਲ ਓ ਬੰਦਿਆ,
ਬੰਦੇ ਪਾਣੀ ਤੇ ਚੱਲਦੇ ਵੇਖੇ।

ਲੋਕੀਂ ਕਹਿੰਦੇ ਦਾਲ ਨੀਂ ਗਲਦੀ,
ਅਸਾਂ ਪੱਥਰ ਗਲਦੇ ਵੇਖੇ,
ਜਿੰਨਾਂ ਕਦਰ ਨਾ ਕੀਤੀ ਯਾਰ ਦੀ ਬੁਲ੍ਹਿਆ
ਹੱਥ ਖ਼ਾਲੀ ਓ ਮਲਦੇ ਵੇਖੇ।

۵.   چڑدے سورج

چڑدے سورج ڈھلدے ویکھے ،
بجے دیوے بلدے ویکھے ،
ہیرے دا کوئی مل نہ تارے،
کھوٹے سکے چلدے ویکھے ۔

جنہاں دا نہ جگ تے کوئی ،
او وی پتّر پلدے ویکھے ،
اودی رحمت نال او بندیا ،
بندے پانی تے چلدے ویکھے ۔

لوگی کہندے دال نئیں گلدی ،
اساں پتھر گلدے ویکھے ،
جناں کدر نہ کیتی یار دی بلھیا ،
ہتھ خالی او ملدے ویکھے ۔

11

6.   Sectarianism (Firka-bundhi).

On one side live Wahhabis, the other Deobandis,

Front and back are Shia and Sunni, strong is sectarianism.

Midst of all this is our house, grim is our fate,

One neighbourhood, eight mosques, which one should we follow!

ਫਿਰਕਾ ਬੰਦੀ

ਇੱਕ ਪਾਸੇ ਰਹਿਨ ਵਹਾਬੀ, ਇਕ ਪਾਸੇ ਦਿਓ ਬੰਦੀ,

ਅੱਗੇ ਪਿੱਛੇ ਸ਼ੀਆ ਸੁੰਨੀ, ਡਾਢੀ ਫਿਰਕਾ ਬੰਦੀ,

ਵਿੱਚ ਵਿਚਾਲੇ ਸਾਡਾ ਕੋਠਾ, ਕਿਸਮਤ ਸਾਡੀ ਮੰਦੀ,

ਇੱਕ ਮਹੱਲਾ, ਅੱਠ ਮਸੀਤਾਂ, ਕਿਹਦੀ ਕਰਾਂ ਪਾਬੰਦੀ।

٦. فرکا بندی

اک پاسے رہن وہابی ، اک پاسے دیوبندی ،

اگے پچھے شیعہ سنی ، ڈاڈھی فرکابندی،

وچ وچالے ساڈھ کوٹھا، کسمت ساڈی مندی،

اک مہلہ، اٹھ مسیتاں، کہیدی کراں پابندی ۔

13

7.   In a single point (Ik nuktay wich).

Grasp the point, let go of the Reckoning,

Cast aside Hell, and tortures of the grave,

Close shut the gateways of unbelief,

Make clean the desires of your heart!

>   In such a house the Word finds refuge,

>   In a single point, the whole discussion is concluded!

Mere prostration, is just rubbing of the ground,

Thus gaining a marked forehead, is for showing off,

Professing the Kalima to please others,

Is not about bringing understanding in your heart!

>   Can the true word ever be hidden?

>   In a single point, the whole discussion is concluded!

One goes to the jungle, another the seas,

Only eating a single grain each day,

Without understanding, tiring their bodies,

Then return home having become sickly.

>   In pointless Retreats, only the body shrivels!

>   In a single point, the whole discussion is concluded!

Grab an able Guide, so Godliness can begin,

Within you be ecstasy and carefreeness,

Without want and in total contentment,

Your heart be full of truth,

>   Bullehya! can the true word ever stop?

>   In a single point, the whole discussion is concluded!

14

ਇੱਕ ਨੁਕਤੇ ਵਿੱਚ

ਫੜ ਨੁਕਤਾ, ਛੋੜ ਹਿਸਾਬਾਂ ਨੂੰ,
ਛੱਡ ਦੋਜ਼ਖ, ਗੋਰ ਅਜ਼ਾਬਾਂ ਨੂੰ,
ਕਰ ਬੰਦ ਕੁਫਰ ਦੀਆਂ ਬਾਬਾਂ ਨੂੰ,
ਕਰ ਸਾਫ ਦਿਲੇ ਦੀਆਂ ਖਾਬਾਂ ਨੂੰ

ਗੱਲ ਏਸੇ ਘਰ ਵਿੱਚ ਢੱਕਦੀ ਏ,
ਇੱਕ ਨੁਕਤੇ ਵਿੱਚ ਗੱਲ ਮੁਕਦੀ ਏ।

ਏਵੇਂ ਮੱਥਾ ਜ਼ਮੀਨ ਘਸਾਈਦਾ,
ਪਾ ਲੰਮਾ ਮਹਿਰਾਬ ਦਿਖਾਈਦਾ,
ਪੜ ਕਲਮਾ ਲੋਕ ਹਸਾਈ ਦਾ,
ਦਿਲ ਅੰਦਰ ਸਮਝ ਨਾ ਲਾਈ ਦਾ,

ਕਦੇ ਸੱਚੀ ਗੱਲ ਵੀ ਲੁੱਕਦੀ ਏ?
ਇੱਕ ਨੁਕਤੇ ਵਿੱਚ ਗੱਲ ਮੁਕਦੀ ਏ

ਇੱਕ ਜੰਗਲ, ਬਹਿਰੀਂ ਜਾਂਦੇ ਨੇਂ,
ਇੱਕ ਦਾਣਾ ਰੋਜ਼ ਦਾ ਖਾਂਦੇ ਨੇਂ
ਬੇ ਸਮਝ ਵਜੂਦ ਥਕਾਂਦੇ ਨੇਂ,
ਘਰ ਆਵਣ ਹਉਕੇ ਮਾਂਦੇ ਨੇਂ,

ਐਵੇਂ ਚਿੱਲਿਆਂ ਅੰਦਰ ਜਿੰਦ ਸੁੱਕਦੀ ਏ।
ਇੱਕ ਨੁਕਤੇ ਵਿੱਚ ਗੱਲ ਮੁੱਕਦੀ ਏ।

ਫੜ ਮੁਰਸ਼ਦ, ਅਬਦ ਖੁਦਾਈ ਹੋ,
ਵਿੱਚ, ਮਸਤੀ ਬੇਪਰਵਾਹੀ ਹੋ,
ਬੇ-ਖਵਾਹਿਸ਼, ਬੇ ਨਵਾਈ ਹੋ,
ਵਿੱਚ ਦਿਲ ਦੇ ਖੂਬ ਸੱਚਾਈ ਹੋ,

ਬੁੱਲ੍ਹਿਆ, ਕਦੀ ਸੱਚੀ ਗੱਲ ਵੀ ਲੁੱਕਦੀ ਏ,
ਇੱਕ ਨੁਕਤੇ ਵਿੱਚ ਗੱਲ ਮੁੱਕਦੀ ਏ।

15

٧.   اک نقطے وچ

پھڑ نقطہ ، چھوڑ حساباں نوں ،

چھڈ دوزخ ، گور عزاباں نوں ،

کر بند کفر دیاں باباں نوں ،

کر صاف دلئے دیاں خاباں نوں ،

گل ایسے گھر وچ ڈھکدی اے،

اک نقطے وچ گل مکدی اے

ایویں متھا زمین گھسائی دا،

پا لما مہرآب دکھائی دا ،

پڑھ کلمہ لوک ہسائی دا ،

دل اندر سمجھ نہ لائی دا،

کدے سچی گل وی لکدی اے ؟

اک نقطے وچ گل مکدی ا

اک جنگل ، بحریں جاندے نیں ،

اک دانا روز دا کھاندے نیں ،

بے سمجھ وجود تھکاندے نیں ،

گھر آون ہو کے ماندے نیں ،

ایویں چلیاں انرر جند سکدی اے۔

اک نکتے وچ گل مکدی اے

پھر مرشد ، ابد خدائی ہو،

وچ ، مستی بے پروائی ہو،

بے خواہش ، بے نوائی ہو،

وچ دل دے خوب سچائی ہو،

بلھیا، کدی سچی گل وی رکدی اے،

اک نکتے وچ گل مکدی اے .

8. The One sitting at home (Ghur bettha).

Reading and reading, you have become a high scholar,

But you have never studied your own self,

You keep rushing into temples and mosques,

But you have never entered your inner self.

For nothing you battle with Satan every day,

When you have never fought your own ego,

Bulleh Shah! you are trying to catch those flying in the heavens,

But you have never grasped the One sitting at home!

ਘਰ ਬੈਠਾ।

ਪੜ੍ਹ ਪੜ੍ਹ ਆਲਮ ਫਾਜ਼ਲ ਹੋਇਆਏਂ,

ਕਦੀ ਆਪਣੇ ਆਪ ਨੂੰ ਪੜ੍ਹਿਆ ਈ ਨਹੀਂ,

ਜਾ ਜਾ ਵੜਨਾ ਏਂ ਮੰਦਰ ਮਸੀਤਾਂ,

ਕਦੇ ਮਨ ਆਪਣੇ ਵਿੱਚ ਵੜਿਆ ਈ ਨਹੀਂ।

ਐਵੇਂ ਰੋਜ਼ ਸ਼ੈਤਾਨ ਨਾਲ ਲੜਨਾ ਏਂ,

ਕਦੀ ਨਫ਼ਸ ਆਪਣੇ ਨਾਲ ਲੜਿਆ ਈ ਨਹੀਂ,

ਬੁਲ੍ਹੇ ਸ਼ਾਹ! ਆਸਮਾਨੀ ਉੱਡਦਿਆਂ ਨੂੰ ਫੜਨਾ ਏਂ,

ਜਿਹੜਾ ਘਰ ਬੈਠਾ ਉਹਨੂੰ ਫੜਿਆ ਈ ਨਹੀਂ।

੮.	ਘਰ ਬੈਠਾ .

پڑھ پڑھ عالم فاضل ہویاں،

کدی اپنڑے آپ نوں پڑھیا ای نہں،

جا جا وڑدا ایں مندر مسیتاں ،

کدی من اپنڑے وچ وڑیا ای نہں -

ایویں روز شیطان نال لڑنا ایں ،

کدی نفس اپنڑے نال لڑیا ای نہں،

بلھے شاہ ! آسمانی اڈیاں پھڑنا ایں ،

جیہڑا گھر بیٹھا اوہنو پھڑیا ای نہں -

9. Bullehya! What I know who I am (Bullehya! Ki jannan main kon).

Not am I a Believer, nor inside mosques,

Not am I in the rituals of the unbelievers,

Not am I in the pure, nor in the un-cleansed,

Not am I Moses, nor am I Pharaoh!

                     Bullehya! what I know who I am.

Not am I in notions of impurity and pureness,

Not in happiness, nor in sorrow,

Not am I of water, nor am I of dust,

Not am I fire, nor within air!

                     Bullehya! what I know who I am.

Not am I in the books of Veda,

Not within opium, nor in alcohol,

Not in the antics of the intoxicated and corrupt,

Not in keeping awake, nor in sleep!

                     Bullehya! what I know who I am.

Not I who founded the mysteries of religion,

Not I who bore Adam and Eve,

Nor have I had Myself named,

Not am I in staying put, nor in wandering,

                     Bullehya! what I know who I am.

I know Myself to be the First and Last,

There is no one else I acknowledge,

There is no one more capable then Me,

Bullehya! who is there left standing?

                     Bullehya! what I know who I am.

ਬੁੱਲ੍ਹਿਆ! ਕੀ ਜਾਨਾਂ ਮੈਂ ਕੌਣ।

ਨਾ ਮੈਂ ਮੋਮਨ, ਵਿੱਚ ਮਸੀਤਾਂ,

ਨਾ ਮੈਂ ਵਿੱਚ ਕੁਫਰ ਦੀਆਂ ਰੀਤਾਂ,

ਨਾ ਮੈਂ ਪਾਕਾਂ, ਵਿੱਚ ਪਲੀਤਾਂ,

ਨਾ ਮੈਂ ਮੂਸਾ, ਨਾ ਫੇਰਉਨ,

ਬੁੱਲ੍ਹਿਆ! ਕੀ ਜਾਨਾਂ ਮੈਂ ਕੌਣ।

ਨਾ ਮੈਂ ਵਿੱਚ ਪਲੀਤੀ ਪਾਕੀ,

ਨਾ ਵਿੱਚ ਸ਼ਾਦੀ, ਨਾ ਗ਼ਮਨਾਕੀ,

ਨਾ ਮੈਂ ਆਬੀ, ਨਾ ਮੈਂ ਖ਼ਾਕੀ,

ਨਾ ਮੈਂ ਆਤਿਸ਼, ਨਾ ਵਿੱਚ ਪੌਣ,

ਬੁੱਲ੍ਹਿਆ! ਕੀ ਜਾਨਾਂ ਮੈਂ ਕੌਣ।

ਨਾ ਮੈਂ ਅੰਦਰ ਵੇਦ ਕਿਤਾਬਾਂ,

ਨਾ ਵਿੱਚ ਭੰਗਾਂ, ਨਾ ਸ਼ਰਾਬਾਂ,

ਨਾ ਵਿੱਚ ਰਿੰਦਾਂ ਮਸਤ ਖਰਾਬਾਂ

ਨਾ ਵਿੱਚ ਜਾਗਨ, ਨਾ ਵਿੱਚ ਸੌਣ,

ਬੁੱਲ੍ਹਿਆ! ਕੀ ਜਾਨਾਂ ਮੈਂ ਕੌਣ।

ਨਾ ਮੈਂ ਭੇਦ ਮਜ਼ਹਬ ਦਾ ਪਾਇਆ,

ਨਾ ਮੈਂ ਆਦਮ ਹਵਾ ਜਾਇਆ,

ਨਾ ਮੈਂ ਅਪਨਾ ਨਾਮ ਧਰਾਇਆ,

ਨਾ ਵਿੱਚ ਬੈਠਣ, ਨਾ ਵਿੱਚ ਭੌਣ,

ਬੁੱਲ੍ਹਿਆ! ਕੀ ਜਾਨਾਂ ਮੈਂ ਕੌਣ।

ਅੱਵਲ ਆਖਰ ਆਪ ਨੂੰ ਜਾਨਾਂ,

ਨਾ ਕੋਈ ਦੂਜਾ ਹੋਰ ਪਛਾਨਾਂ,

ਮੈਥੋਂ ਵੱਧ ਨਾ ਕੋਈ ਸਿਆਨਾ,

ਬੁੱਲ੍ਹਿਆ! ਉਹ ਕਿਹੜਾ ਹੈ ਕੌਣ?

ਬੁੱਲ੍ਹਿਆ! ਕੀ ਜਾਨਾਂ ਮੈਂ ਕੌਣ।

۹.			بلھیا ! کی جاناں میں کون

نہ میں مومن ، وچ مسیتاں ،

نہ میں وچ کفر دیاں ریتاں،

نہ میں پاکاں ، وچ پلیتاں،

نہ میں موسیٰ، نہ فرعون ،

بلھیا ! کی جاناں میں کون ۔

نہ میں وچ پلیتی پاکی ،

نہ وچ شادی ، نہ غمناکی،

نہ میں آبی، نہ میں خاکی ،

نہ میں آتش ، نہ وچ پون ،

بلھیا ! کی جاناں میں کون ۔

نہ میں اندر وید کتاباں ،

نہ وچ بھنگاں، نہ شراباں ،

نہ وچ رنداں مست خراباں،

نہ وچ جاگن، نہ وچ سون ،

بلھیا ! کی جاناں میں کون

نہ میں بھید مذہب دا پایا

نہ میں آدم حوا جایا،

نہ میں اپنا نام دھرایا،

نہ وچ بیٹھن، نہ وچ بھون ،

بلھیا ! کی جاناں میں کون -

اول آخر آپ نوں جاناں ،

نہ کوئی دوجا ہور پچھاناں،

مہتھوں ودھ نہ کوئی سیاناں،

بلھیا ! اوہ کھڑا ہے کون ؟

بلھیا ! کی جاناں میں کون -

10. Dogs are higher than you! (Kuttay tehthoon uttay!)

You awake nights, and declare yourself a Shaikh,

Awake every night are dogs: they are higher then you!

From barking, their mouths never shut,

Then they sleep on rubbish heaps: they are higher then you!

The doorway of their master they never desert,

Though they be beaten: they are higher then you!

Bulleh Shah! You acquire some good deeds too,

Otherwise, the dogs have won the game: they are higher then you!

ਕੁੱਤੇ ਤੈਥੋਂ ਉੱਤੇ

ਰਾਤੀਂ ਜਾਗੀਂ, ਸ਼ੇਖ ਸਦਾਵੇਂ,
ਰਾਤੀਂ ਜਾਗਣ ਕੁੱਤੇ : ਤੈਥੋਂ ਉੱਤੇ।

ਭੱਕਣ ਥੂੰ ਬੰਦ ਮੂਲ ਨਾ ਹੁੰਦੇ,
ਜਾ ਰੋੜੀ ਤੇ ਸੁੱਤੇ : ਤੈਥੋਂ ਉੱਤੇ।

ਖਸਮ ਆਪਣੇ ਦਾ ਦਰ ਨਾ ਛੱਡਦੇ,
ਭਾਵੇਂ ਵੱਜਣ ਜੁੱਤੇ : ਤੈਥੋਂ ਉੱਤੇ।

ਬੁੱਲ੍ਹੇ ਸ਼ਾਹ! ਕੋਈ ਰਿਖਤ ਵਿਹਾਜ ਲੈ,
ਨਹੀਂ ਤਾਂ ਬਾਜ਼ੀ ਲੈ ਗਏ ਕੁੱਤੇ : ਤੈਥੋਂ ਉੱਤੇ।

۱۰.   کتّے تیتھوں اتّے

راتیں جاگیں ، شیخ سدھاویں،
راتیں جاگن کتّے : تیتھوں اتّے !

بھونکن تھوں بند مؤل نہ ہوندے ،
جا روڑی تے ستّے : تیتھوں اتّے !

کھصم اپنے دا در نہ چھڈّے،
پھاویں وجن جتّے : تیتھوں اتّے !

بلھے شاہ ! کوئی رخت ویہاج لے ،
نہیں تے بازی لے گۓ کتّے : تیتھوں اتّے !

11.   Inside and out (Undher, baaher).

Don't keep losing your temper,

Let things cool before eating,

Your days too, will swing around,

Don't fret for no reason!

Sow plants of such love,

That provide shade for the whole village,

Destroy falsehood from within yourself,

Always beat the drum of truth!

Having eaten scraps of food,

Prostrate yourself in humble gratitude,

Sweep your inner self with a broom,

Cleanse your inside and out!

అందర్ బాహర ।

ਗੁੱਸੇ ਵਿੱਚ ਨਾ ਆਇਆ ਕਰ,

ਠੰਢਾ ਕਰ ਕੇ ਖਾਇਆ ਕਰ,

ਦਿਨ ਤੇਰੇ ਵੀ ਫਿਰ ਜਾਣਗੇ,

ਐਵੇਂ ਨਾ ਘਬਰਾਇਆ ਕਰ।

ਪਿਆਰ ਦੇ ਐਸੇ ਬੂਟੇ ਲਾ,

ਸਾਰੇ ਪਿੰਡ ਤੇ ਸਾਇਆ ਕਰ,

ਅਪਨੇ ਅੰਦਰੋਂ ਝੂਠ ਮੁਕਾ,

ਸੱਚ ਦਾ ਢੋਲ ਵਜਾਇਆ ਕਰ।

ਰੁੱਖੀ ਸੁੱਖੀ ਖਾ ਕੇ ਤੂੰ,

ਸੱਜਦੇ ਵਿੱਚ ਟੁਰ ਜਾਇਆ ਕਰ,

ਮਨ ਅੰਦਰ ਤੂੰ ਝਾੜੂ ਦੇ,

ਅੰਦਰ ਬਾਹਰ ਸਫਾਇਆ ਕਰ।

١١.   اندر باہر -

غصے وچ نہ آیا کر ،

ٹھنڈا کر کے کھایا کر ،

دن تیرے وی پھر جان گے ،

اینویں نہ گھبرایا کر۔

پیار دے ایسے بوٹے لا ،

سارے پنڈ تے سایہ کر ،

اپنے اندروں جھوٹ مکا ،

سچ دا ڈھول وجایا کر۔

رکھی سکھی کھا کے توں،

سجدے وچ ٹرجایا کر ،

من اندر توں جھاڑو دے ،

اندر باہر صفایا کر۔

12. Neither am I Hindu, nor Muslim (Hindu nah, naahin Mussalman).

Neither am I Hindu, nor a Muslim,

Lose all your pride in the flowing rivers.

Neither Sunni , nor are we Shia,

 Love for all, is the path we have adopted.

Neither hungry, nor are we sated,

Neither naked, nor are we covered.

Neither weeping, nor are we laughing,

Neither abandoned, nor are we wedded.

Neither sinners, nor are we unblemished,

Path of sinful belief, we do not know.

Bulleh Shah! When loss and defeat is inflicted,

Hindu and Muslim, both suffer alike!

ਹਿੰਦੂ ਨਾ, ਨਾਹੀਂ ਮੁਸਲਮਾਨ

ہندو نہ ، ناہیں مسلمان

ਹਿੰਦੂ ਨਾ, ਨਾਹੀਂ ਮੁਸਲਮਾਨ,
ਬਹੇ ਤ੍ਰਿੰਜਣ, ਤਜ ਅਭਿਮਾਨ ।

ਸੁੰਨੀ ਨਾ, ਨਾਹੀਂ ਹਮ ਸ਼ੀਆ,
ਸੁਲ੍ਹਾ ਕੁੱਲ ਕਾ ਮਾਰਗ ਲੀਆ ।

ਭੁੱਖੇ ਨਾ, ਨਾਹੀਂ ਹਮ ਰੱਜੇ,
ਨੰਗੇ ਨਾ, ਨਾਹੀਂ ਹਮ ਕੱਜੇ ।

ਰੋਂਦੇ ਨਾ, ਨਾਹੀਂ ਹਮ ਹੱਸਦੇ,
ਉਜੜੇ ਨਾ, ਨਾਹੀਂ ਹਮ ਵੱਸਦੇ ।

ਪਾਪੀ ਨਾ, ਸੁਧਰਮੀ ਨਾਂ,
ਪਾਪ ਪੁੰਨ ਕੀ ਰਾਹ ਨਾ ਜਾਨ

ਬੁੱਲ੍ਹੇ ਸ਼ਾਹਾ ਜੋ ਹਰਿ ਚਿਤ ਲਾਗੇ,
ਹਿੰਦੂ ਤੁਰਕ, ਦੂਜਨ ਤਿਆਗੇ ।

ہندو نہ ، ناہیں مسلمان ،
بہے ترنجن، تج ابھماں ۔

سنی نہ ، ناہیں ہم شیعا ،
صلح کل کا مارگ لیا ۔

بھکھے نہ ، ناہیں ہم رجے ،
ننگے نہ ، ناہیں ہم کجے ۔

روندے نہ ، ناہیں ہم ہسدے ،
اجڑے نہ ، ناہیں ہم وسدے ۔

پاپی نہ ، سدھرمی ناں ،
پاپ پن کی راہ نہ جان ۔

بلھے شاہ ! جو ہرچت لاگے ،
ہندو، ترک ، دوجن تیاگے ۔

13. Going to Mecca (Mukkay gaiyan).

Going to Mecca, does not end the matter,

Even if we return having prayed hundreds of Friday prayers!

Going to the Ganges, does not end the matter,

Even if we submerge ourselves hundreds of times!

Going to Gyan, does not end the matter,

Even if we have hundreds of prayers chanted there!

Bulleh Shah! the matter can only end,

When we lose the "Me" from our hearts!

ਮੱਕੇ ਗਿਆਂ

ਮੱਕੇ ਗਿਆਂ ਗੱਲ ਮੁੱਕਦੀ ਨਾਹੀਂ,

ਭਾਵੇਂ ਸੌ ਸੌ ਜੁੰਮੇ ਪੜ੍ਹ ਆਈਏ।

ਗੰਗਾ ਗਿਆਂ ਗੱਲ ਮੁੱਕਦੀ ਨਾਹੀਂ,

ਭਾਵੇਂ ਸੌ ਸੌ ਗੋਤੇ ਖਾਈਏ।

ਗਇਆ ਗਇਆਂ ਗੱਲ ਮੁੱਕਦੀ ਨਾਹੀਂ,

ਭਾਵੇਂ ਸੌ ਸੌ ਪੰਡ ਪੜ੍ਹਾਈਏ।

ਬੁੱਲ੍ਹੇ ਸ਼ਾਹ! ਗੱਲ ਤਾਹੀਂ ਮੁੱਕਦੀ,

ਜਦੋਂ "ਮੈਂ" ਨੂੰ ਦਿਲੋਂ ਗਵਾਈਏ।

مگّے گیاں   ۱۳.

مگّے گیاں گل مگّدی ناہیں ،

پھویں سو سو جمھے پڑھ آئیے -

گنگا گیاں گل مگّدی ناہیں ،

پھویں سو سو غوطے کھایئے۔

گّیا گیاں گل مگّدی ناہیں ،

پھویں سو سو پنڈّھ پڑھایئے -

بلھے شاہ ! گل تہیوں مگّدی ،

جدوں "میں" نوں دلوں گوایئے

14. It is just You! (Tuhiyoon ain!)

It is just You, there's no me, my friend,

It is just You, there's no me!

An image of an empty ruin, my mind is no longer spinning,

If I speak, You speak with me, if I stay silent, my mind does not!

If I sleep, You sleep with me, if I walk You are the way,

Bullehya! My Love has come into my house, my life I give as offering to Him!

It is just You, there's no me, my friend,

It is just You, there's no me!

ਤੂੰਹੀਓਂ ਏਂ।

ਤੂੰਹੀਓਂ ਏਂ, ਮੈਂ ਨਾਹੀਂ, ਸੱਜਣਾ,

ਤੂੰਹੀਓਂ ਏਂ, ਮੈਂ ਨਾਹੀਂ।

ਖੋਲੇ ਦੇ ਪਰਛਾਵੇਂ ਵਾਂਡੂ, ਘੁਮ ਰਹਿਆ ਮਨ ਨਾਹੀਂ,
ਜੇ ਬੋਲਾਂ ਤੂੰ ਨਾਲੇ ਬੋਲੇਂ, ਚੁੱਪ ਰਵਾਂ ਮਨ ਨਾਹੀਂ,
ਜੇ ਸੌਂਵਾਂ ਤਾਂ ਨਾਲੇ ਸੌਂਵੇਂ , ਜੇ ਟੁਰਾਂ ਤੂੰ ਰਾਹੀਂ,
ਬੁੱਲ੍ਹਾ ਸ਼ਹੁ ਘਰ ਆਇਆ ਸਾਡੇ, ਜਿੰਦੜੀ ਘੋਲ ਘੁਮਾਈਂ ।

۱٤. توہیوں ایں -

ਤੂੰਹੀਓਂ ਏਂ, ਮੈਂ ਨਾਹੀਂ, ਸੱਜਣਾ,

ਤੂੰਹੀਓਂ ਏਂ, ਮੈਂ ਨਾਹੀਂ।

توہیوں ایں ، میں ناہیں، سجنا ،

توہیوں ایں ، میں ناہیں !

کھولے دے پرچھاویں وانگوں ، گھوم رہیا من ناہیں ،

جے بولاں توں نالے بولیں ، چپ رھواں من ناہیں ،

جے سونواں توں نالے سونویں ، جے ٹران توں راہیں،

بلھیا ! شوہ گھر آیا میرے، جندڑی گھول گھماہیں -

توہیوں ایں ، میں ناہیں ، سجنا ،

توہیوں ایں ، میں ناہیں !

33

15.   Raze the temple (Mandir dha dai).

Raze the temple, raze the mosque,

Raze whatever can be toppled,

Only, never break a person's heart,

For God resides within hearts!

ਮੰਦਰ ਢਾਹ ਦੇ

ਮੰਦਰ ਢਾਹ ਦੇ, ਮਸਜਿਦ ਢਾਹ ਦੇ,

ਢਾਹ ਦੇ ਜੋ ਕੁਝ ਢਹਿੰਦਾ,

ਇਕ, ਬੰਦੇ ਦਾ ਦਿਲ ਨਾ ਢਾਹਵੀਂ,

ਕੇ ਰੱਬ ਦਿਲਾਂ ਵਿੱਚ ਰਹਿੰਦਾ।

۱۵.   مند ر ڈھا دے

مند ر ڈھا دے ، مسجد ڈھا دے ،
ڈھا دے جو کج ڈھیندھا،
اک ، بندے دا دل نہ ڈھاونیں،
کے رب دلاں وچ رہیندھا !

16.   Enough of your learning, o friend! (Ilmoon bus kurrin o yaar!)

Enough of your learning, o friend, an 'Alif ' is all you require!

The amount of knowledge is infinite,

Your lifetime ending is uncertain,

An 'Alif ' is all you require,

Enough of your learning o friend!

Enough of your learning, o friend!

Reading and writing, you create heaps,

Mounds of books are all around you,

Surrounding you is moonlight, but inside is darkness,

Ask for the "way" and you have no notion!

Enough of your learning, o friend!

You spend your prayers by adding extras,

Loud are your calls to prayer,

You climb the pulpit to shout out sermons,

Knowledge has ruined you!

Enough of your learning, o friend!

Doctrine has created more differences,

Those with eyes are totally blind,

They seize the innocent and spare the thief,

In both Worlds may they be losers!

Enough of your learning, o friend!

Reading much, you have yourself proclaimed a scholar,

You make up complex edicts sitting at home,

You feed off the loot from the ignorant,

You turn false oaths into true!

Enough of your learning, o friend!

Reading much, mullah becomes a judge,

God is pleased even without such learning,

But your greed refreshes day by day,

You have been ruined by your greed!

Enough of your learning, o friend!

You relish recounting religious conundrums,

You eat the food earned of suspicion and doubt,

You say one thing but do another,

Within you is falseness, outside is piety!

Enough of your learning, o friend!

When I learnt the lesson of True Love,

Seeing the river of Universal Unity, I entered,

I got stuck in the swirling currents of confusion,

Shah Innayat brought me across!

Enough of your learning, o friend!

An 'Alif' is all you require!

ਇਲਮੋਂ ਬੱਸ ਕਰੀਂ ਓ ਯਾਰ

ਇਲਮੋਂ ਬੱਸ ਕਰੀਂ ਓ ਯਾਰ, ਇੱਕੋ ਅਲਫ਼ ਤੇਰੇ ਦਰਕਾਰਾ।

ਇਲਮ ਨਾ ਆਵੇ ਵਿਚ ਸੁਮਾਰ,
ਜਾਂਦੀ ਉਮਰ, ਨਹੀਂ ਇਤਬਾਰ,

ਇੱਕੋ ਅਲਫ਼ ਤੇਰੇ ਦਰਕਾਰ

ਇਲਮੋਂ ਬੱਸ ਕਰੀਂ ਓ ਯਾਰ,
                    ਇਲਮੋਂ ਬੱਸ ਕਰੀਂ ਓ ਯਾਰ।

ਪੜ੍ਹ ਪੜ੍ਹ, ਲਿਖ ਲਿਖ, ਲਾਵੇਂ ਢੇਰ,

ਢੇਰ ਕਿਤਾਬਾਂ ਚਾਰ ਚੁਫੇਰ,
ਗਿਰਦੇ ਚਾਨਣ, ਵਿਚ ਅਨ੍ਹੇਰ,

ਪੁੱਛੇ "ਰਾਹ" ਤੇ ਖਬਰ ਨਾ ਸਾਰ ।
                    ਇਲਮੋਂ ਬੱਸ ਕਰੀਂ ਓ ਯਾਰ।

ਪੜ੍ਹ ਪੜ੍ਹ ਨਫ਼ਲ, ਨਮਾਜ਼ ਗੁਜ਼ਾਰੋਂ,

ਉੱਚੀਆਂ ਬਾਂਗਾਂ ਚਾਂਘਾਂ ਮਾਰੋਂ,
ਮਿੰਬਰ ਤੇ ਚੜ੍ਹ ਵਾਅਜ਼ ਪੁਕਾਰੋਂ,

ਕੀਤਾ ਤੈਨੂੰ ਇਲਮ ਖੁਆਰ ।
                    ਇਲਮੋਂ ਬੱਸ ਕਰੀਂ ਓ ਯਾਰ।

ਇਲਮੋਂ ਪਏ ਕਿਜ਼ੀਏ ਹੋਰ,

ਅੱਖਾਂ ਵਾਲੇ ਅੰਨ੍ਹੇ ਕੋਰ,
ਫੜਕੇ ਸਾਧ ਤੇ ਛੱਡੇ ਚੋਰ,

ਦੋਹੀਂ ਜਹਾਨੀਂ ਹੋਣ ਖ਼ੁਆਰ ।

       ਇਲਮੋਂ ਬੱਸ ਕਰੀਂ ਓ ਯਾਰ।

ਪੜ੍ਹ ਪੜ੍ਹ ਸ਼ੇਖ ਮਸ਼ਾਇਖ ਕਹਾਵੇਂ,

ਉਲਟੇ ਮਸਲੇ ਘਰੋਂ ਬਣਾਵੇਂ,
ਬੇ-ਇਲਮਾਂ ਨੂੰ ਲੁਟ ਲੁਟ ਖਾਵੇਂ,

ਝੂਠੇ ਸੱਚੇ ਕਰੋਂ ਇਕਰਾਰ ।

       ਇਲਮੋਂ ਬੱਸ ਕਰੀਂ ਓ ਯਾਰ।

ਪੜ੍ਹ ਪੜ੍ਹ ਮੁੱਲਾਂ ਹੋਇ ਕਾਜ਼ੀ,

ਅੱਲਾਹ ਇਲਮਾ ਬਾਹਝੋਂ ਰਾਜ਼ੀ,
ਹੋਵੇ ਹਿਰਸ ਦਿਨੇ ਦਿਨ ਤਾਜ਼ੀ,

ਤੈਨੂੰ ਕੀਤਾ ਹਿਰਸਾਂ ਖ਼ੁਆਰ ।

       ਇਲਮੋਂ ਬੱਸ ਕਰੀਂ ਓ ਯਾਰ।

ਪੜ੍ਹ ਪੜ੍ਹ ਮਸਲੇ ਪਿਆ ਸੁਣਾਵੇਂ,

ਖਾਣਾ ਸ਼ੱਕ ਸ਼ਬਹੇ ਦਾ ਖਾਵੇਂ,
ਦੱਸੇਂ ਹੋਰ, ਤੇ ਹੋਰ ਕਮਾਵੇਂ,

ਅੰਦਰ ਖੋਟ, ਬਾਹਰ ਸਚਿਆਰ ।

       ਇਲਮੋਂ ਬੱਸ ਕਰੀਂ ਓ ਯਾਰ।

ਜਦ ਮੈਂ ਸਬਕ ਇਸ਼ਕ ਦਾ ਪੜ੍ਹਿਆ,

ਦਰਿਆ ਵੇਖ ਵਹਦਤ ਦਾ ਵੜਿਆ,
ਘੁੰਮਣ ਘੇਰਾਂ ਦੇ ਵਿਚ ਅੜਿਆ,

ਸ਼ਾਹ ਇਨਾਇਤ ਲਾਇਆ ਪਾਰ ।

       ਇਲਮੋਂ ਬੱਸ ਕਰੀਂ ਓ ਯਾਰ।

       ਇੱਕੋ ਅਲਫ਼ ਤੇਰੇ ਦਰਕਾਰ।

١٦.   علموں بس کریں او یار

علموں بس کریں او یار ، اکو الف ترے درکار !

علم نہ آوے وچ شمار ،

جاندی عمر، نہیں اعتبار،

اکو الف ترے درکار،

علموں بس کریں او یار،

علموں بس کریں او یار !

پڑھ پڑھ ، لکھ لکھ ، لاویں ڈھیر،

ڈھیر کتاباں چار چوفیر،

گردہے چانن، وچ انھیر،

پچھو " راہ " تے خبر نہ سار،

علموں بس کریں او یار !

پڑھ پڑھ نفل ، نماز گزاریں،

اچیاں بانگاں چھانگھاں ماریں ،

منبر تے چڑ وعظ پکاریں ،

کیتا تینوں علم خوار ،

علموں بس کریں او یار !

علموں پئے قضیے ہور،

اگھاں والے آنھے کوڑھ،

پھڑدے سادھ تے چھڈن چور،

دوہیں جہانیں ہون خوار،

علموں بس کریں او یار!

پڑھ پڑھ شیخ مشائخ کہاویں،

الٹے مسلئے گھروں بناویں،

بے علماں نوں لٹ لٹ کھاویں،

چھوٹھے سچے کریں اقرار،

علموں بس کریں او یار !

پڑھ پڑھ ملاں ہوے قاضی،

اللہ علماں باجھوں راضی،

ہووے ہرص دنوں دن تازی،

تینوں کیتا ہرص خوار،

علموں بس کریں او یار !

پڑھ پڑھ مسلئے پیا سناویں،

کھانا شک شبھے دا کھاویں،

دسیں ہور، تے ہور کماویں،

اندھر کھوٹ، باہر سچیار،

41

علموں بس کریں او یار !

جد میں سبق عشق دا پڑھیا،

دریا ویکھ وحدت دا وڑیا ،

گھمن گھیراں دے وچ اڑیا،

شاہ عنایت لایا پار!

علموں بس کریں او یار!

اکو الف ترے درکار !

17.   Some ask! (Koi puccho!)

Some ask, "why does the Sweetheart do this?"

> Whatever He does, so He does!

In the mosque, He spends ritual prayers,

> then shows up in the temple!

Himself alone, yet of millions of homes,

> He is the Master of each one!

By dwelling happily in just one house,

> He cannot stay veiled!

Whomever I look at, He is there,

> He accompanies everyone!

In the river of Universal Oneness, can be seen,

> This entire world floating!

Bullehya! the love of my Master is cunning,

> it enters by blood and grazes on the flesh!

Some ask, " why does the Sweetheart do this?"

> Whatever He does, so He does!

ਕੋਈ ਪੁੱਛੇ।

ਕੋਈ ਪੁੱਛੇ "ਦਿਲਬਰ ਕੀ ਕਰਦਾ?" "ਇਹ ਜੋ ਕਰਦਾ ਸੋ ਕਰਦਾ!"

ਵਿਚ ਮਸੀਤ ਨਮਾਜ਼ ਗੁਜ਼ਾਰੇ, ਬੁੱਤਖ਼ਾਨੇ ਜਾ ਵੜਦਾ ।

ਆਪ ਇੱਕੇ, ਕਈ ਲੱਖ ਘਰਾਂ ਦੇ, ਮਾਲਕ ਹੈ ਘਰ ਘਰ ਦਾ ।
ਇਕਸੇ ਘਰ ਵਿਚ ਰਸਦੇ ਵਸਦੇ, ਨਹੀਂ ਰਹਿੰਦਾ ਵਿਚ ਪਰਦਾ ।
ਜਿਤ ਵੱਲ ਵੇਖਾਂ, ਉੱਤ ਵੱਲ ਓਹੋ, ਹਰ ਦੀ ਸੰਗਤ ਕਰਦਾ ।
ਵਹਿਦਤ ਦੇ ਦਰਿਆ ਦੇ ਅੰਦਰ ਸਭ ਜਗ ਦਿੱਸੇ ਤਰਦਾ।

ਬੁੱਲ੍ਹਿਆ! ਸ਼ਹੁ ਦਾ ਇਸ਼ਕ ਬਘੇਲਾ, ਰੱਤੀਂ ਪੀਂਦਾ, ਗੋਸ਼ਤ ਚਰਦਾ ।

ਕੋਈ ਪੁੱਛੇ ਦਿਲਬਰ ਕੀ ਕਰਦਾ? ਇਹ ਜੋ ਕਰਦਾ ਸੋ ਕਰਦਾ।

۱۷.   کوئی پچھو -

کوئی پچھو" دلبرکی کردا ؟ " " ایہ جو کردا سو کردا ! "

وچ مسیت نماز گزارے، بتخانے جا وڑدا ۔

آپ اکو، کئی لکھ گھراں دے، مالک ہے گھر گھر دا ۔

اکسے گھر وچ رسدے وسدے نابیں رہندا وچ پردا ۔

جت ول ویکھاں، ات ول اوہو، ہر دی سنگت کردا ۔

و حدت دے دریا دے اندر سب جگ دسے تردا۔

بلھیا ! شوہ دا عشق بگھیلا، رتیں پیندا، گوشت چردا۔

کوئی پچھو دلبر کی کردا ؟ ایہ جو کردا سو کردا !

18.   What repentance? (Kaissi toba?)

What repentance is this repentance? Don't repent like this my friend!

Repentance is on your lips, but not coming from your heart,

From such repentance, you don't give up your ways,

What ignorance has veiled you from seeing,

Why would the All-forgiving, give you forgiveness?

                        Don't repent like this my friend!

He gives us a coarse beggar's cloak,

To get one-up on the rich and powerful,

How can he attain Muslim attributes,

He who has such a character?

                        Don't repent like this my friend!

Where forbidden, there you go,

You consume by deceit, what rightfully belongs to others,

A hundred books you carry on your head,

How can you even be trusted?

                        Don't repent like this my friend!

Oppressors are not afraid of oppressing,

They die of their own doings,

Neither do they have fear of God,

Here, there, they be disgraced!

                        Don't repent like this my friend!

What repentance is this repentance? Don't repent like this my friend!

ਕੈਸੀ ਤੋਬਾ

ਕੈਸੀ ਤੋਬਾ ਹੈ ਇਹ ਤੋਬਾ, ਐਸੀ ਤੋਬਾ ਨਾ ਕਰ ਯਾਰ!

ਮੂੰਹੋ ਤੋਬਾ ਦਿਲੋਂ ਨਾ ਕਰਦਾ,
ਇਸ ਤੋਬਾ ਥੀਂ ਤਰਕ ਨਾ ਫੜਦਾ,
ਕਿਸ ਗਫਲਤ ਨੇ ਪਾਇਓ ਪੜਦਾ,
ਤੈਨੂੰ ਬਖਸ਼ੇ ਕਿਉਂ ਗਾਫਾਰ?
                ਐਸੀ ਤੋਬਾ ਨਾ ਕਰ ਯਾਰ!
ਸਾਨੂੰ ਦੇ ਕੇ ਲੈਈ ਸਵਾਏ,
ਡਾਢਿਆਂ ਉੱਤੇ ਬਾਜ਼ੀ ਲਾਏ,
ਮੁਸਲਮਾਨੀ ਉਹੋ ਕਿਥੋਂ ਪਾਏ,
ਜਿਸ ਦਾ ਹੋਵੇ ਇਹ ਕਿਰਦਾਰ?
                ਐਸੀ ਤੋਬਾ ਨਾ ਕਰ ਯਾਰ!
ਜਿਤ ਨਾ ਜਾਣਾ ਉੱਥੇ ਜਾਵੇਂ,
ਹੱਕ ਬੇਗਾਨਾ ਮੁੱਕਰ ਖਾਵੇਂ,
ਕੋੜ ਕਿਤਾਬਾਂ ਸਿਰ ਤੇ ਚਾਵੇਂ,
ਹੋਵੇ ਕੀ ਤੇਰਾ ਇਤਬਾਰ?
                ਐਸੀ ਤੋਬਾ ਨਾ ਕਰ ਯਾਰ!
ਜ਼ਾਲਮ ਜ਼ੁਲਮੋ ਨਾਹੀਂ ਡਰਦੇ,
ਆਪਨੀ ਕੀਤੀਓ ਆਪੇ ਮਰਦੇ,
ਨਾਹੀਂ ਖੋਫ ਖ਼ੁਦਾ ਦਾ ਕਰਦੇ,
ਇੱਥੇ ਉੱਥੇ ਹੋਣ ਖ਼ੁਆਰ।
                ਐਸੀ ਤੋਬਾ ਨਾ ਕਰ ਯਾਰ!
ਕੈਸੀ ਤੋਬਾ ਹੈ ਇਹ ਤੋਬਾ, ਐਸੀ ਤੋਬਾ ਨਾ ਕਰ ਯਾਰ!

کیسی توبا ہے ایہ توبا ، ایسی توبا نہ کر یار!

مونھوں توبا ، دلوں نہ کردا،

اس توبا تھیں ترک نہ پھڑدا،

کس غفلت نے پایو پڑدا،

تینوں بخشے کیوں غفار؟

ایسی توبا نہ کر یار !

سانوں دے کے لؤی سوائے،

ڈاہڈیاں آتے بازی لائے،

مسلمانی اوہ کتھوں پائے،

جس دا ہووے ایہ کردار؟

ایسی توبا نہ کر یار !

جت نہ جانا ، اوتھے جاویں،

حق بیگانا مگر کھاویں،

کوڑ کتاباں سر تے چاویں،

ہووے کی تیرا اعتبار ؟

ایسی توبا نہ کر یار !

ظالم ظلموں نہیں ڈردے،

اپنی کیتیوں آپے مردے ،

نہیں خوف خدا دا کردے ،

ایتھے اوتھے ہون خوار!

ایسی توبا نہ کر یار !

کیسی توبا ہے ایہ توبا ، ایسی توبا نہ کر یار!

19. Accomplished Teacher (Kamil Murshid).

People keep urging Bulleh,

you go and pray in the mosque!

Within mosques what can happen,

if the prayer is not intended from your heart?

What can happen from external ablutions,

if impurity remains within?

Without an accomplished Teacher, Bullehya,

for nothing is gone your performed worship!

ਕਾਮਲ ਮੁਰਸ਼ਦ

ਬੁੱਲ੍ਹੇ ਨੂੰ ਲੋਕੀ ਮੱਤੀ ਦਿੰਦੇ,
ਤੂੰ ਜਾ ਬਹੁ ਮਸੀਤੀ।

ਵਿੱਚ ਮਸੀਤਾਂ ਕੀ ਕੁੱਝ ਹੁੰਦਾ,
ਜੇ ਦਿਲੋਂ ਨਮਾਜ਼ ਨਾ ਨੀਤੀ।

ਬਾਹਰੋਂ ਪਾਕ ਕੀਤੇ ਕੀ ਹੁੰਦਾ,
ਜੇ ਅੰਦਰੋ ਨਾ ਗਈ ਪਲੀਤੀ?

ਬਿਣ ਕਾਮਲ ਮੁਰਸ਼ਦ ਬੁੱਲ੍ਹਿਆ,
ਤੇਰੀ ਐਵੇਂ ਗਈ ਇਬਾਦਤ ਕੀਤੀ।

١٩.   کامل مرشد

بلھے نوں لوک متیں دیندے ،
توں جا بہو مسیتی !

وچ مسیتاں کیہ کجھ ہوندا،
جے دلوں نماز نہ نیتی !

باہروں پاک کیتے کیہ ہوندا ،
جے اندروں نہ گئی پلیتی ؟

بن کامل مرشد بلھیا ،
تیری ایویں گئی عبادت کیتی !

20.   Just chant Alif (Ik Alif purrho!)

Just chant Alif, it is a release for you!

From one Alif became two, three, and four,

They then became thousands of millions,

From there, they became uncountable,

The point of this Alif is unique,

> Just chant Alif, it is a release for you!

Why have you become the image of executioners,

Why are you reading lorry-loads of books,

Weighing down on your head, bundles of torment,

For the way ahead is difficult and hard,

> Just chant Alif, it is a release for you!

Without an expert teacher, you memorize the Quran,

You keep uttering prayers to cleanse your speech,

But your focus is on your own benefit,

Your mind is spinning like a circular saw,

> Just chant Alif, it is a release for you!

ਇੱਕ ਅਲਫ਼ ਪੜ੍ਹੋ

ਇਕ ਅਲਫ਼ ਪੜ੍ਹੋ ਛੁੱਟਕਾਰਾ ਏ।

ਇਕ ਅਲਫ਼ੋਂ, ਦੋ, ਤਿੰਨ, ਚਾਰ ਹੋਏ,
ਫਿਰ ਲੱਖ ਕਰੋੜ ਹਜ਼ਾਰ ਹੋਏ,
ਫਿਰ ਉਥੇਂ ਬਾਝ ਸੁਮਾਰ ਹੋਏ,
ਏਸ ਅਲਫ਼ ਦਾ ਨੁਕਤਾ ਨਿਆਰਾ ਏ,
                    ਇਕ ਅਲਫ਼ ਪੜ੍ਹੋ ਛੁੱਟਕਾਰਾ ਏ ।
ਕਿਉ ਹੋਇਆ ਏ ਸ਼ਕਲ ਜੱਲਾਦਾਂ ਦੀ,
ਕਿਉਂ ਪੜ੍ਹਨਾ ਏਂ ਗੱਡ ਕਿਤਾਬਾਂ ਦੀ,
ਸਿਰ ਚਾਨਾਂ ਏ ਪੰਡ ਅਜ਼ਾਬਾਂ ਦੀ,
ਅੱਗੇ ਪੈਂਡਾ ਮੁਸ਼ਕਲ ਭਾਰਾ ਏ,
                    ਇਕ ਅਲਫ਼ ਪੜ੍ਹੋ ਛੁੱਟਕਾਰਾ ਏ ।
ਬਿਣ ਹਾਫ਼ਜ਼ ਹਿਫ਼ਜ਼ ਕੁਰਾਨ ਕਰੇਂ,
ਪੜ੍ਹ ਪੜ੍ਹ ਕੇ ਸਾਫ਼ ਜ਼ਬਾਨ ਕਰੇਂ,
ਪਰ ਨਹਿਮਤ ਵਿੱਚ ਧਿਆਨ ਕਰੇਂ,
ਮਨ ਫਿਰਦਾ ਜਿਉਂ ਹਲਕਾਰਾ ਏ,
                    ਇਕ ਅਲਫ਼ ਪੜ੍ਹੋ ਛੁੱਟਕਾਰਾ ਏ ।

۲۰.   اک الف پڑھو

اک الف پڑھو، چھٹکارا اے ۔

اک الفوں، دو ، تن ، چار ہوئے ،

فر لکھ کروڑ ہزار ہوئے ،

فر اوتھوں باجھ شمار ہوئے ،

ایس الف دا نکتا نیارا اے ،

اک الف پڑھو چھٹکارا اے ۔

کیوں ہویا ایس شکل جلاداں دی ،

کیوں پڑھنا ایس گڈھ کتاباں دی ،

سر چاناں ایس پنڈھ عزاباں دی ،

اگے پینڈا مشکل پھارا اے،

اک الف پڑھو چھٹکارا اے ۔

بن حافظ حفظ قرآن کریں،

پڑھ پڑھ کے صاف زبان کریں ،

پر نعمت وچ دھیان کریں ،

من پھردا جیوں ہلکارا اے ،

اک الف پڑھو چھٹکارا اے

54

21.   Let it be (Bus kar ji).

Let it be, now let it be,

Just one thing, live with us happily!

You reside within my heart,

For what then do you run away from me,

Yet, with powerful magic you tug my heart,

Let it be, now let it be!

You were beating ones, who were already dead,

Like Kaidho, you were battering us,

You were strangling the necks of those speaking up,

Now hit us with well-aimed arrows!

Let it be, now let it be!

You are trying to hide, but we have caught you,

We have tied you up with a lock of hair,

You are still looking for ways to disappear,

Now, there is no escape by running away!

Let it be, now let it be!

Bulleh, my Master, I am your slave,

I am dying to see your face,

I beseech you countless times,

Now come and sit deep in my chest!

Let it be, now let it be!

ਬੱਸ ਕਰ ਜੀ

ਬੱਸ ਕਰ ਜੀ, ਹੁਣ ਬੱਸ ਕਰ ਜੀ,
ਇਕ ਬਾਤ ਅਸਾਂ ਨਾਲ ਹੱਸ ਕਰ ਜੀ ।

ਸੀਂ ਦਿਲ ਮੇਰੇ ਵਿਚ ਵੱਸਦੇ ਓ
ਐਵੇਂ ਸਾਥੋਂ ਦੂਰ ਕਿਉਂ ਨੱਸਦੇ ਓ,
ਨਾਲੇ ਘੱਤ ਜਾਦੂ ਦਿਲ ਖੱਸਦੇ ਓ,
ਹੁਣ ਕਿਤ ਵੱਲ ਜਾਸੇ ਨੱਸ ਕਰ ਜੀ ।
        ਬੱਸ ਕਰ ਜੀ, ਹੁਣ ਬੱਸ ਕਰ ਜੀ ।
ਸੀਂ ਮੋਇਆਂ ਨੂੰ ਮਾਰ ਮੁਕੰਦੇ ਸੀ,
ਨਿੱਤ ਕੋਦੇ ਵਾਂਗ ਕੁਟੰਦੇ ਸੀ,
ਗੱਲ ਕਰਦਿਆਂ ਦਾ ਗਲਾ ਘੁੱਟੰਦੇ ਸੀ,
ਹੁਣ ਤੀਰ ਲਗਾਵੇ ਕੱਸ ਕਰ ਜੀ ।
        ਬੱਸ ਕਰ ਜੀ, ਹੁਣ ਬੱਸ ਕਰ ਜੀ ।
ਸੀਂ ਛਪਦੇ ਓ, ਅਸਾਂ ਪਕੜੇ ਓ,
ਅਸਾਂ ਨਾਲ ਜ਼ੁਲਫ ਦੇ ਜਕੜੇ ਓ,
ਸੀਂ ਅਜੇ ਛਪਣ ਤੋਂ ਤਕੜੇ ਓ,
ਹੁਣ ਜਾਣ ਨਾ ਮਿਲਦਾ ਨੱਸ ਕਰ ਜੀ,
        ਬੱਸ ਕਰ ਜੀ, ਹੁਣ ਬੱਸ ਕਰ ਜੀ ।
ਬੁੱਲ੍ਹੇ, ਸ਼ੌਹ ਮੈਂ ਤੇਰੀ ਬਰਦੀ ਆਂ,
ਤੇਰਾ ਮੁੱਖ ਵੇਖਣ ਨੂੰ ਮਰਦੀ ਆਂ,
ਨਿੱਤ ਸੈ ਸੈ ਮਿੰਨਤਾਂ ਕਰਦੀ ਆਂ,
ਹੁਣ ਬੈਠ ਪਿੰਜਰ ਵਿਚ ਧੱਸ ਕਰ ਜੀ ।
        ਬੱਸ ਕਰ ਜੀ ਹੁਣ ਬੱਸ ਕਰ ਜੀ ।

بس کر جی ، ہن بس کر جی ،

اک بات اساں نال ہس کر جی ۔

سیں دل میرے وچ وسدے او ،

ایویں ساتھیوں دور کیوں نسدے او ،

نالے گھت جادو دل کھسدے او ،

بس کر جی ، ہن بس کر جی ۔

سیں موئیاں نوں مار مکیندے سی ،

نت کیدھو وانگ کٹیندے سی ،

گل کردیاں دا گلا گھٹیندے سی ،

ہن تیر لگاوو کس کر جی ،

بس کر جی ، ہن بس کر جی ۔

سیں چھپدے او، اساں پکڑے او ،

اساں نال زلف دے جکڑے او ،

سیں اجیں چھپن توں تکڑے او ،

ہن جاں نہ ملدا نس کر جی ،

بس کر جی، ہن بس کر جی ۔

بلھے ، شوہ میں تیری بردی اں،

تیرا مکھ ویکھن نوں مردی اں،

نت سو سو منتاں کردی اں ،

ہن بیٹھ پنجرو چ دھس کر جی ،

بس کر جی ، ہن بس کر جی ۔

22.   The nature of God and man (Rab tai bundhay di zaat).

The nature of God and man is one,

Like the nature of cloth is fibre,

God is hidden such, within man,

Like fibre is hidden within cloth.

He Himself calls, and Himself answers,

Himself He says "Hoon",

If an accomplished Teacher is found Bullehya,

Then there is no " me" left and no "you"!

ਰੱਬ ਤੇ ਬੰਦੇ ਦੀ ਜ਼ਾਤ

ਰੱਬ ਤੇ ਬੰਦੇ ਦੀ ਜ਼ਾਤ ਇੱਕੋ,
ਜਿਵੇਂ ਕੱਪੜੇ ਦੀ ਜ਼ਾਤ ਏ ਤੂੰ,
ਰੱਬ ਬੰਦੇ ਵਿੱਚ ਇੰਜ ਲੁਕਿਆ,
ਜਿਵੇਂ ਕੱਪੜੇ ਵਿੱਚ ਲੁਕਿਆ ਏ ਤੂੰ।

ਆਪ ਬੁਲਾਵੇ, ਤੇ ਆਪੇ ਹੀ ਬੋਲੇ,
ਆਪੇ ਹੀ ਕਰਦਾ ਏ "ਹੂੰ",
ਕਾਮਲ ਮੁਰਸ਼ਦ ਮਿਲ ਜਾਏ ਬੁੱਲ੍ਹਿਆ,
ਤੇ ਨਾ "ਮੈਂ" ਰਹੇ ਨਾ "ਤੂੰ"।

٢٢.   رب تے بندے دی ذات

رب تے بندے دی ذات اکو ،
جیویں کپڑے دی ذات اے روں،
رب بندے وچ انج لکیا ،
جیویں کپڑے وچ لکیا اے روں ۔

آپ بلاوے ، تے آپے ہی بولے ،
آپے ہی کردا اے "ہوں" ،
کامل مرشد مل جائے بلھیا ،
تے نہ "میں" رہیے ، تے نہ " توں" ۔

61

23. White or black (Gori ya kaali).

Someone asked of Mian Majnu,

But your Laila is of a dark complexion,

Mian Majnu answered him thus,

Your eye is not capable of seeing!

The pages of the holy Quran are white,

On them, the writing is with black ink,

Leave it Bullehya, when you have given your heart,

Then so what if she's white or she's black!

गोरी या काली

किसे कीता सवाल मिआं मजनूं नूं,
तेरी लैला ते रंग दी काली ए,
दित्ता जवाब मिआं मजनूं ने,
तेरी अॅख ना वेखण वाली ए।

कुरान पाक दे वरक ने चिॅटे,
अते लिखी सिआह काली ए,
छॅड वे बुॅलिआ, दिल दे छडिआ,
ते फिर की गोरी, ते की काली ए।

گوری یا کالی   ۲۳.

کسے کیتا سوال میاں مجنوں نوں ،
تیری لیلیٰ تے رنگ دی کالی اے ،
دتا جواب میاں مجنوں نے،
تیری اکھ نہ ویکھن والی اے ۔

قرآن پاک دے ورق نے چٹے،
اَتے لگّھی سیاہی کالی اے ،
چھڈ وے بلھیا ، دل دے چھڈیا،
تے فر کی گوری ، تے کی کالی اے ۔

24. Wake up! (Utth jaag!)

Wake up! Stop your snoring, this slumber is no use for you!

Where now is Alexander the Great? Death spares not saint nor prophet,

All have left their piles of ruins, no-one here is everlasting!

Whatever you do, so you will get, otherwise you will regret in the end,

Like a lonely crane you will shriek, for without feathers there is no flight!

Bulleh! Without the Master there is no-one, here, there, in either inn,

Take each step with great care, for you will not return a second time!

Wake up! Stop your snoring, this slumber is no use for you!

ਉੱਠ ਜਾਗਾ!

ਉੱਠ ਜਾਗ ਘੁਰਾੜੇ ਮਾਰ ਨਹੀਂ, ਇਹ ਸੌਨ ਤੇਰੇ ਦਰਕਾਰ ਨਹੀਂ।

ਕਿੱਥੇ ਹੈ ਸੁਲਤਾਨ ਸਿਕੰਦਰ? ਮੌਤ ਨਾ ਛੱਡੇ ਪੀਰ ਪੈਗ਼ੰਬਰ
ਸਭੇ ਛੱਡ ਛੱਡ ਗਏ ਅਡੰਬਰ, ਕੋਈ ਏਥੇ ਪਾਏਦਾਰ ਨਹੀਂ।

ਜੋ ਕੁਝ ਕਰਸੇਂ ,ਸੋ ਕੁਝ ਪਾਸੇਂ, ਨਹੀਂ ਤੇ ਓੜਕ ਪੁੱਛੇ ਤਾਸੇਂ,
ਸੁੰਝੀ ਕੂੰਜ ਵਾਂਗੂੰ ਕੁਰਲਾ ਸੇਂ, ਖੰਬਾਂ ਬਾਝ ਉਡਾਰ ਨਹੀਂ

ਬੁੱਲ੍ਹੇ! ਸ਼ਹੁ ਬਿਨ ਕੋਈ ਨਾਹੀਂ, ਏਥੇ ਓਥੇ ਦੋਈਂ ਸਰਾਈਂ
ਸੰਭਲ ਸੰਭਲ ਕਦਮ ਟਿਕਾਈਂ, ਫਿਰ ਆਵਣੂ ਦੂਜੀ ਵਾਰ ਨਹੀਂ

ਉੱਠ ਜਾਗ ਘੁਰਾੜੇ ਮਾਰ ਨਹੀਂ, ਇਹ ਸੌਨ ਤੇਰੇ ਦਰਕਾਰ ਨਹੀਂ।

اٹھ جاگ گھڑ اڑے مار نہیں ، ایہ سون ترے درکار نہیں ۔

کتھے ہے سلطان سکندر؟ موت نہ چھڈے پیر پیغمبر ،
سبھے چھڈ چھڈ گئے اڈمبر، کوئی ایتھے پائندار نہیں ۔

جو کجھ کرسیں ، سو کجھ پاسیں، نہیں تے اوڑک پچھتاسیں،
سونجھی کونج ونگوں کرلاسیں ، کھنباں باجھ اڈار نہیں ۔

بلھے ! شوہ بن کوئی نا ہیں ، ایتھے اوتھے دوئیں سراہیں ،
سنبھل سنبھل کدم ٹکائیں، پھیر آون دوجی وار نہیں ۔

اٹھ جاگ گھڑ اڑے مار نہیں ، ایہ سون ترے درکار نہیں ۔

25.   Take out this timekeeper! (Ghurryali daiwo nikaal ni!)

Take out this timekeeper,

My precious sweetheart has come home!

This clock keeps beating second by second,

Thus shortening this night of our union,

If it could understand my mind's desire,

It would throw away this clock with his own hands!

Take out this timekeeper!

Never-ending, beautiful music is now playing,

The musician! Handsome, and his harmony so perfect,

Forgotten have I fasts, prayers and rituals,

Now, the bartenders are offering goblets of wine!

Take out this timekeeper!

All my sorrow and grief has been lifted,

When I saw His face, it was a wondrous sight,

The night is passing, do something to prolong it,

Put up a wall infront of the coming day!

Take out this timekeeper!

Bullehya! the Master's abode I adore,

Without being able to swim, I have floated,

So, so rarely has my turn arrived,

That parting now is unbearable!

Take out this timekeeper,

My precious sweetheart has come home!

ਘੜਿਆਲੀ ਦਿਉ ਨਿਕਾਲ ਨੀ।

ਘੜਿਆਲੀ ਦਿਉ ਨਿਕਾਲ ਨੀ,
ਮੇਰਾ ਪੀ ਘਰ ਆਇਆ, ਲਾਲ ਨੀ ।

ਘੜੀ ਘੜੀ ਘੜਿਆਲ ਬਜਾਵੇ,
ਰੈਣ ਵਸਲ ਦੀ ਪਿਆ ਘਟਾਵੇ,
ਮੇਰੇ ਮਨ ਦੀ ਬਾਤ ਜੋ ਪਾਵੇ,
ਹੱਥੋਂ ਚਾ ਸੁੱਟੇ ਘੜਿਆਲ ਨੀ ।

ਘੜਿਆਲੀ ਦਿਉ ਨਿਕਾਲ ਨੀ।

ਅਨਹਦ ਬਾਜਾ ਬਜੇ ਸੁਹਾਨਾ,
ਮੁਤਰਿਬਾ ਸੁਖੜਾ ਤਾਨ ਤਰਾਨਾ,
ਭੁੱਲਾ ਸੋਮ, ਸਲਾਤ ਦੁਗਾਨਾ,
ਮਯ ਪਿਆਲਾ ਦੇਨ ਕਲਾਲ ਨੀ ।

ਘੜਿਆਲੀ ਦਿਉ ਨਿਕਾਲ ਨੀ।

ਦੁੱਖ ਦਲਿਦਰ ਉੱਠ ਗਿਆ ਸਾਰਾ,
ਮੁਖ ਵੇਖਿਆ ਤੇ ਅਜਬ ਨਜ਼ਾਰਾ,
ਰੈਣ ਵਧੀ ਕੁਝ ਕਰੋ ਪਸਾਰਾ,
ਦਿਨ ਅੱਗੇ ਧਰੋ ਦੀਵਾਲ ਨੀ ।

ਘੜਿਆਲੀ ਦਿਉ ਨਿਕਾਲ ਨੀ।

ਬੁਲ੍ਹਿਆ ਸ਼ਹੁ ਦੀ ਸੇਜ ਪਿਆਰੀ,
ਨੀ ਮੈਂ ਤਾਰਨਹਾਰੇ ਤਾਰੀ,
ਕਿਵੇਂ ਕਿਵੇਂ ਮਿਰੀ ਆਈ ਵਾਰੀ,
ਹੁਣ ਵਿਛੜਨ ਹੋਇਆ ਮੁਹਾਲ ਨੀ ।

ਘੜਿਆਲੀ ਦਿਉ ਨਿਕਾਲ ਨੀ।

گھڑیالی دیو نکال نی ،

میرا پیا گھر آیا ، لعل نی ۔

گھڑی گھڑی گھڑیال بجاوے ،

رین وصل دی پیا گھٹاوے ،

میرے من دی بات جے پاوے ،

ہتھوں چا سٹّے گھڑیال نی ،

گھڑیالی دیو نکال نی ۔

انہد باجا بجے سہانا ،

مطرب ! سگھڑا تان ترانا ،

بھلا صوم ، صلات دوگانہ ،

مدھ پیالہ دین کلال نی ،

گھڑیالی دیو نکال نی ۔

دکھ دلدر اٹھ گیا سارا ،

مکھ ویکھیا تے عجب نظارا ،

رین ودھی، کجھ کرو پسارا ،

دن اگے دھرو دیوال نی ،

گھڑیالی دیو نکال نی ۔

بلھیا! شوہ دی سیج پیاری ،

نی میں تار نیہارے تاری،

کویں کویں مری آئی واری ،

ہن وچھڑن ہویا مہال نی ،

گھڑیالی دیونکال نی ۔

میرا پیا گھر آیا۔

26.   Difficult! (Okha!)

Fool..., to earn true love is difficult!

Making someone your true friend is difficult!

Love, love, everyone bellows,

Having loved, fulfilling it is difficult!

Anyone can laugh at others' misfortunes,

Sharing someone's sorrow is difficult!

Words alone do not gain a Sufi's station,

Changing into a wanderer's guise is difficult!

Bullehya! no one listens to what someone says,

Making people understand is difficult!

ਔਖਾ

ਝੱਲਿਆ.., ਇਸ਼ਕ ਕਮਾਣਾ ਔਖਾ,
ਕਿਸੇ ਨੂੰ ਯਾਰ ਬਣਾਣਾ ਔਖਾ।

ਪਿਆਰ ਪਿਆਰ ਤੇ ਹਰ ਕੋਈ ਕੂਕੇ,
ਕਰਕੇ ਪਿਆਰ, ਨਿਭਾਉਣਾ ਔਖਾ।

ਹਰ ਕੋਈ ਦੁੱਖਾਂ ਤੇ ਹੱਸ ਲੈਂਦਾ,
ਕਿਸੇ ਦਾ ਦਰਦ ਵੰਡਾਉਣਾ ਔਖਾ।

ਗੱਲਾਂ ਨਾਲ ਨਹੀਂ ਸੂਫੀ ਰੁਤਬੇ ਮਿਲਦੇ,
ਜੋਗੀ ਭੇਸ ਵਟਾਉਣਾ ਔਖਾ,

ਕੋਈ ਕਿਸੇ ਦੀ ਗਲ ਨਹੀਂ ਸੁਣਦਾ,
ਲੋਕਾਂ ਨੂੰ ਸਮਝਾਉਣਾ ਔਖਾ।

٢٦.   اوکھا

جھلیا..، عشق کمانا اوکھا ،
کسے نوں یار بنانا اوکھا ۔

پیار پیار تے ہر کوئی کوکے ،
کر کے پیار، نبھانا اوکھا ۔

ہر کوئی دکھاں تے ہنس لیندا،
کسے دا درد ونڈھؤنا اوکھا ۔

گلاں نال نہیں صوفی رتبے ملدے ،
جوگی بھیس وٹاؤنا اوکھا ۔

کوئی کسے دی گل نہیں سندا،
لوکاں نوں سمجھانا اوکھا ۔

27.   Birds. (Punchi).

Consider o' man, the birds flying in the sky,

Just reflect on what they do.

Neither do they hoard food,

Nor do they die of starvation!

Has anyone ever seen these winged creatures,

Starving to death?

Only mankind hoards food,

And it is people who die of hunger!

ਪੰਛੀ।

ਵੇਖ ਬੰਦਿਆ ਅਸਮਾਨਾ ਉੱਡਦੇ ਪੰਛੀ,
ਵੇਖ ਤੇ ਸਹੀ ਕੀ ਕਰਦੇ ਨੇ,
ਨਾ ਓ ਕਰਦੇ ਰਿਜ਼ਕ ਜ਼ਖੀਰਾ,
ਨਾ ਓ ਭੁੱਖੇ ਮਰਦੇ ਨੇ।

ਕਦੀ ਕਿਸੇ ਨੇ ਪੰਖ ਪਖੇਰਾ,
ਭੁੱਖੇ ਮਰਦੇ ਵੇਖੇ ਨੇ?
ਬੰਦੇ ਹੀ ਕਰਦੇ ਰਿਜ਼ਕ ਜ਼ਖੀਰਾ,
ਬੰਦੇ ਹੀ ਭੁੱਖੇ ਮਰਦੇ ਨੇ।

٢٧.   پنچھی -

ویکھ بندیا اسماناں اڈدے پنچھی ،
ویکھ تے سہی کی کردے نے ،
نہ او کردے رزق ذخیرہ ،
نہ او بھکھے مردے نے -

کدی کسے نیں پنکھ پکھیرہ ،
بھکھے مردے ویکھے نے ؟
بندے ہی کردے رزق ذخیرہ ،
بندے ہی بھکھے مردے نے !

28.   Faith in One God (Tawheed).

Being learned, does not make noble,

Those who are genuinely base,

Brass can never be turned to gold,

Even if it is set with rubies and diamonds!

A miser can never give alms,

Though he has millions in treasure,

Bullehya! without faith in one God, Paradise will not be gained,

Even if we were to die in holy Medina!

ਤੌਹੀਦ।

ਇਲਮ ਪੜ੍ਹਿਆਂ ਅਸ਼ਰਾਫ ਨਾ ਹੋਵਣ,
ਜਿਹੜੇ ਹੋਵਣ ਅਸਲ ਕਮੀਨੇ,
ਪਿੱਤਰ ਕਦੀ ਨਹੀਂ ਸੋਨਾ ਬਣਦਾ,
ਭਾਵੇਂ ਜੜੀਏ ਲਾਲ ਨਗੀਨੇ।

ਸ਼ੋਮ ਬੀ ਕਦੀ ਨਹੀਂ ਸਦਕਾ ਹੁੰਦਾ,
ਭਾਵੇਂ ਹੋਵਣ ਲੱਖ ਖਜ਼ੀਨੇ,
ਬੁੱਲ੍ਹਿਆ! ਬਾਝ ਤੌਹੀਦ ਜੰਨਤ ਨਹੀਂ ਮਿਲਦੀ,
ਭਾਵੇਂ ਮਰੀਏ ਵਿੱਚ ਮਦੀਨੇ।

٢٨.   توحید -

علم پڑھیاں اشرآف نہ ہوون،

جھیڑے ہوون اصل کمینے ،

پتل کدی نہیں سونا بن دا،

پھویں جڑیہے لعل نگینے -

شوم تھیں کدی نہیں صدقہ ہوندا،

پھویں ہوون لکھ خزینے ،

بلھیا ! بھاج توحید نہیں جنت ملنی ،

پھویں مریے وچ مد ہینے -

77

29.   I am without confines! (Main bay-kaidh!)

I am without confines, I am without bounds,

> Neither am I afflicted, nor am I the healer!

Not am I a Believer, nor am I a heathen,

> Neither am I a Sayyid, nor am I a commoner!

By fourteen generations are we descended,

> Nowhere can we be confined!

In the lowly is our life,

> In that, there is no doubt nor fault!

Why are you questioning the caste of Bulleh Shah?

> It neither exists, nor is desirable!

I am without confines, I am without bounds!

ਮੈਂ ਬੇ ਕੈਦ।

ਮੈਂ ਬੇ-ਕੈਦ ਆਂ, ਮੈਂ ਬੇ-ਕੈਦ, ਨਾ ਰੋਗੀ ਨਾ ਵੈਦ ।

ਨਾ ਮੈਂ ਮੋਮਨ, ਨਾ ਮੈਂ ਕਾਫ਼ਰ, ਨਾ ਸੈਦ ਨਾ ਸਜ਼ੀਏਦ ।

ਚੰਦੀ ਤਬਕੀ ਸੀਰ ਅਸਾਡਾ, ਕਿਤੇ ਨਾ ਹੋਵੇ ਕੈਦ ।

ਖ਼ਰਾਬਾਤ ਮੇਂ ਜਾਲ ਅਸਾਡੀ, ਨਾ ਸ਼ੋਭਾ ਨਾ ਐਬ ।

ਬੁੱਲ੍ਹੇ ਸ਼ਾਹ ਦੀ ਜ਼ਾਤ ਕੀ ਪੁਛਨੀ ਐਂ? ਨਾ ਪੈਦਾ ਨਾ ਪੈਦ ।

ਮੈਂ ਬੇ-ਕੈਦ ਆਂ, ਮੈਂ ਬੇ-ਕੈਦ।

٢٩.		میں بے قید ۔

میں بے قید آں، میں بے قید ، نہ روگی نہ وید ۔

نہ میں مومن ، نہ میں کافر، نہ سید نہ سیدھ ۔

چودھیں طبقیں سیرا ساڈا، کتے نہ ہوویئے قید ۔

خرابات میں جال اساڈی، نہ شوبھا نہ عیب ۔

بلھے شاہ دی ذات کی پچھنی ایں؟ نہ پیدا ناپید۔

میں بے قید آں، میں بے قید ۔

30. Ranjha, Ranjha. (Ranjha, Ranjha).

Chanting Ranjha, Ranjha, now I have myself become Ranjha,

Forever now, see me as Ranjha, no one call me Heer!

Ranjha is within me, I am within Ranjha, no other thoughts occur to us,

There is no me, it is all Him, this is how He amuses Himself.

Whatever shows from within us, that is our nature,

 The one with whom I have become enamoured, I have become like him.

Take off the white shawl o maiden, put on the wanderers' blanket,

The white shawl will become stained, the blanket shows no stains.

Take me to Takht Hazaaray Bullehya, in Siyaal I find no peace,

Chanting Ranjha, Ranjha, now I have myself become Ranjha.

ਰਾਂਝਾ ਰਾਂਝਾ।

ਰਾਂਝਾ ਰਾਂਝਾ ਕਰਦੀ ਹੁਣ ਮੈਂ ਆਪੇ ਰਾਂਝਾ ਹੋਈ,
ਸੱਦੋ ਮੈਨੂੰ ਧੀਦੋ ਰਾਂਝਾ, ਹੀਰ ਨਾ ਆਖੋ ਕੋਈ ।

ਰਾਂਝਾ ਮੈਂ ਵਿੱਚ, ਮੈਂ ਰਾਂਝੇ ਵਿੱਚ, ਗ਼ੈਰ ਖ਼ਿਆਲ ਨਾ ਕੋਈ ।
ਮੈਂ ਨਹੀਂ, ਉਹ ਆਪ ਹੈ, ਆਪਣੀ ਆਪ ਕਰੇ ਦਿਲਜੋਈ ।

ਜੋ ਕੁਝ ਸਾਡੇ ਅੰਦਰ ਦਿੱਸੇ, ਜਾਤ ਅਸਾਡੀ ਸੋਈ,
ਜਿਸ ਦੇ ਨਾਲ ਮੈਂ ਨੇਹੁੰ ਲਗਾਇਆ, ਉਹੋ ਜੈਸੀ ਹੋਈ।

ਚਿੱਟੀ ਚਾਦਰ ਲਾਹ ਸੁੱਟ ਕੁੜੀਏ, ਪਹਿਨ ਫਕੀਰਾਂ ਲੋਈ,
ਚਿੱਟੀ ਚਾਦਰ ਦਾਗ਼ ਲਗੋਸੀ, ਲੋਈ ਦਾਗ਼ ਨਾ ਕੋਈ।

ਤਖਤ ਹਜ਼ਾਰੇ ਲੈ ਚੱਲ ਬੁੱਲ੍ਹਿਆ, ਸਿਆਲੀਂ ਮਿਲੇ ਨਾ ਢੋਈ,
ਰਾਂਝਾ ਰਾਂਝਾ ਕਰਦੀ ਹੁਣ ਮੈਂ ਆਪੇ ਰਾਂਝਾ ਹੋਈ।

رانجھا رانجھا کردی ہن میں آپے رانجھا ہوئی ،
سدو مینوں دیدو رانجھا، ہیر نہ آکھو کوئی ۔

رانجھا میں وچ ، میں رانجھے وچ، غیر خیال نہ کوئی ،
میں نہیں، اوہ آپ ہے، اپنی آپ کرے دلجوئی ۔

جو کجھ سـاڈے اندر د سـے، ذات اسـاڈی سوہی ،
جس دے نال میں نیونھ لگایا ، اوہو جیسی ہوئی ۔

چٹی چادر لاہ سٹ کڑیے، پہن فقیراں لوئی،
چٹی چادر داغ لگیسی، لوئی داغ نہ کوئی ۔

تہخت ہزارے لے چل بلھیا، سیالیں ملے نہ ڈھوئی،
رانجھا رانجھا کردی ہن میں آپے رانجھا ہوئی ۔

31. Haji folk (Haji lok).

Haji folk go to Mecca,

My soulmate Ranjha is my Mecca,

O I'm a fool!

I am betrothed to my love Ranjha,

But my father is trying to deceive me,

O I'm a fool!

Haji folk go to Mecca,

In my heart are nine hundred Meccas,

O I'm a fool!

Amongst them are Hajis, amongst them Qazis,

Amongst them are thieves and tricksters,

O I'm a fool!

Haji folk go to Mecca,

We will go to Takht Hazzarah,

O I'm a fool!

Whichever direction is the Beloved, that way is the Kaaba,

Even if you search through the four Holy Books!

O I'm a fool!

ਹਾਜੀ ਲੋਕ ਮੱਕੇ ਨੂੰ ਜਾਂਦੇ

ਹਾਜੀ ਲੋਕ ਮੱਕੇ ਨੂੰ ਜਾਂਦੇ,
ਮੇਰਾ ਰਾਂਝਾ ਮਾਹੀ ਮੱਕਾ,

   ਨੀ ਮੈਂ ਕਮਲੀ ਆਂ।
ਮੈਂ ਮੰਗ ਰਾਂਝੇ ਯਾਰ ਦੀ ਹੋਈਆਂ,
ਮੇਰਾ ਬਾਬਲ ਕਰਦਾ ਧੱਕਾ,

   ਨੀ ਮੈਂ ਕਮਲੀ ਆਂ ।
ਹਾਜੀ ਲੋਕ ਮੱਕੇ ਵੱਲ ਜਾਂਦੇ,
ਮੇਰੇ ਘਰ ਵਿਚ ਨੈਸੋਹ ਮੱਕਾ,

   ਨੀ ਮੈਂ ਕਮਲੀ ਆਂ।

ਵਿਚੇ ਹਾਜੀ ਵਿਚੇ ਕਾਜ਼ੀ,
ਵਿਚੇ ਚੋਰ ਉਚੱਕਾ,

   ਨੀ ਮੈਂ ਕਮਲੀ ਆਂ।
ਹਾਜੀ ਲੋਕ ਮੱਕੇ ਵੱਲ ਜਾਂਦੇ,
ਅਸਾਂ ਜਾਣਾ ਤਖ਼ਤ ਹਜ਼ਾਰੇ,

   ਨੀ ਮੈਂ ਕਮਲੀ ਆਂ।
ਜਿਤ ਵੱਲ ਯਾਰ, ਉਤੇ ਵੱਲ ਕਾਅਬਾ,
ਭਾਵੇਂ ਫੋਲ ਕਿਤਾਬਾਂ ਚਾਰੇ,

   ਨੀ ਮੈਂ ਕਮਲੀ ਆਂ।

حاجی لوک مگّے ول جاندے ،

میرا رانجھا ماہی مگّے،

نی میں کملی اں !

میں منگ رانجھے یار دی ہویاں،

میرا بابل کردا دھگّا،

نی میں کملی اں !

حاجی لوک مگّے ول جاندے ،

میرے گھر وچ نو سو مگّے،

نی میں کملی اں !

وچے حاجی ، وچے قاضی ،

وچے چور اچکا،

نی میں کملی اں !

حاجی لوک مگّے ول جاندے ،

اساں جاناں تخت ہزارے ،

نی میں کملی اں !

جت ول یار، اتّے ول کعبہ،

پھویں پھول کتاباں چارے ۔

نی میں کملی اں !

32.   Such perverse times have come (Ultay hor zummanay ayai).

Such perverse times have come,

That I have been able to learn the secrets of the Beloved.

Crows have started killing falcons, and sparrows have downed hawks,

Horses graze from rubbish heaps and donkeys are being fed horseweed.

There is no love between relations, whether be maternal or paternal uncles,

No unity between father and sons or with daughters, their mothers.

Honest people are getting pushed away, while liars are being sat close,

The heirs have been bankrupted, the followers are now holding court.

Sackcloth wearers have been made Rajahs, the Rajahs made to beg,

Bullehya! the order has come from the Supreme , who can turn this away?

Such perverse times have come,

That I have been able to learn the secrets of the Beloved.

ਉਲਟੇ ਹੋਰ ਜ਼ਮਾਨੇ ਆਏ

ਉਲਟੇ ਹੋਰ ਜ਼ਮਾਨੇ ਆਏ, ਤਾਂ ਮੈਂ ਭੇਦ ਸੱਜਣ ਦੇ ਪਾਏ।

ਕਾਂ ਲਗੜਾਂ ਨੂੰ ਮਾਰਨ ਲੱਗੇ, ਚਿੜੀਆਂ ਜੱਰੇ ਢਾਏ,
ਘੋੜੇ ਚੁਗਣ ਅਰੂੜੀਆਂ 'ਤੇ ਗੱਦੋਂ ਖਵੇਦ ਪਵਾਏ।

ਆਪਣਿਆਂ ਵਿਚ ਉਲਫ਼ਤ ਨਾਹੀਂ, ਕੇ ਚਾਚੇ ਕੇ ਤਾਏ,
ਪਿਉ ਪੁੱਤਰਾਂ ਇਤਫ਼ਾਕ ਨਾ ਕਾਹੀ, ਧੀਆਂ ਨਾਲ ਨਾ ਮਾਏ।

ਸੱਚਿਆਂ ਨੂੰ ਪਏ ਮਿਲਦੇ ਧੱਕੇ, ਝੂਠੇ ਕੋਲ ਬਹਾਏ,
ਅਗਲੇ ਹੋ ਕੰਗਾਲੇ ਬੈਠੇ, ਪਿਛਲਿਆਂ ਫ਼ਰਸ਼ ਵਿਛਾਏ।

ਬੋੜਿਆਂ ਵਾਲੇ ਰਾਜੇ ਕੀਤੇ, ਰਾਜਿਆਂ ਭੀਖ ਮੰਗਾਏ,
ਬੁਲ੍ਹਿਆ! ਹੁਕਮ ਹਜ਼ੂਰੋਂ ਆਇਆ, ਤਸ ਨੂੰ ਕੋਣ ਹਟਾਏ।

ਉਲਟੇ ਹੋਰ ਜ਼ਮਾਨੇ ਆਏ, ਤਾਂ ਮੈਂ ਭੇਦ ਸੱਜਣ ਦੇ ਪਾਏ।

الٹے ہور زمانے آۓ، تاں میں بھید سجن دے پاۓ ۔

کاں لگڑاں نوں مارن لگّے، چڑیاں جرّے ڈھاۓ،
گھوڑے چگن اروڑیاں تے گدّھوں خوید پوواۓ ۔

آپنیاں وچ الفت ناہیں، کیہ چاچے کیہ تاۓ،
پیو پتراں اتفاق نہ کاہی، دھیاں نال نہ ماۓ ۔

سچیاں نوں پۓ ملدے دھگّے، جھوٹھے کول بہاۓ،
اگلے ہو کنگالے بیٹھے، پھچھلیاں فرش وچھاۓ ۔

بوریاں والے راجے کیتے، راجیاں بھیک منگاۓ،
بلھیا! حکم حضوروں آیا، تس نوں کون ہٹاۓ ۔

الٹے ہور زمانے آۓ ، تاں میں بھید سجن دے پاۓ ۔

33. Now, who are You hiding Yourself from? (Hunh kis thin aap chuppai dha?)

Somewhere you teach Sunnah and religious obligations, somewhere you are the Mullah saying the call to prayer,

Somewhere you are professing Ram, somewhere you are applying the tilak mark to your forhead,

Now, who are You hiding yourself from?

Somewhere you are a thief, somewhere the Qazi, somewhere you climb the pulpit and give sermons,

Somewhere you are Tegh Bahadur Ghazi, upon yourself , charging an army,

Now, who are you hiding yourself from?

You adopt many different guises, the wine You drink all to Yourself,

To me, you are visible everywhere, You Yourself are carrying it all,

Now, who are you hiding yourself from?

The one who searches for You, he is dead before dying,

Even in death he is afraid of You, the dead are never brought back,

Now, who are you hiding yourself from?

"Consciousness", is it mine or is it Yours? In the end it is a mound of dust,

This mound of dust my Beloved has surrounded, this pile of dust is being made to dance,

Now, who are You hiding Yourself from?

Bullah! now you really understand the Master, you can recognise Him by His features,

Somewhere You are coming, somewhere You are going, now I will not be able to forget You,

Now, who are you hiding yourself from?

ਹੁਣ ਕਿਸ ਥੀਂ ਆਪ ਛੁਪਾਈਦਾ?

ਕਿਤੇ ਸੁੰਨਤ ਫ਼ਰਜ਼ ਦਸੇਂਦੇ ਓ, ਕਿਤੇ ਮੁੱਲਾਂ ਬਾਂਗ ਬੁਲੇਂਦੇ ਓ,

ਕਿਤੇ ਰਾਮ ਦੁਹਾਈ ਦੇਂਦੇ ਓ, ਕਿਤੇ ਮੱਥੇ ਤਿਲਕ ਲਗਾਈਦਾ,

> ਹੁਣ ਕਿਸ ਥੀਂ ਆਪ ਛੁਪਾਈਦਾ ?

ਕਿਤੇ ਚੋਰ ਓ, ਕਿਧਰੇ ਕਾਜ਼ੀ ਓ, ਕਿਤੇ ਮਿੰਬਰ ਤੇ ਬਹਿ ਵਾਅਜ਼ੀ ਓ,

ਕਿਤੇ ਤੇਗ਼ ਬਹਾਦਰ ਗ਼ਾਜ਼ੀ ਹੋ, ਆਪੇ ਪਰ ਕਟਕ ਚੜ੍ਹਾਈਦਾ,

> ਹੁਣ ਕਿਸ ਥੀਂ ਆਪ ਛੁਪਾਈਦਾ?

ਤੁਸੀਂ ਸਭਨੀਂ ਭੇਸੀਂ ਥੀਂਦੇ ਓ, ਮਦ ਆਪੇ ਆਪੇ ਪੀਂਦੇ ਓ,

ਮੈਨੂੰ ਹਰ ਜਾ ਤੁਸੀਂ ਦਸੀਂਦੇ ਓ, ਆਪੇ ਕੋ ਆਪ ਚੁਕਾਈਦਾ,

> ਹੁਣ ਕਿਸ ਥੀਂ ਆਪ ਛੁਪਾਈਦਾ?

ਜੋ ਚੁੰਘ ਤੁਸਾਡੀ ਕਰਦਾ ਐ, ਮੋਇਆਂ ਤੋਂ ਅੱਗੇ ਮਰਦਾ ਐ,

ਮੋਇਓਂ ਵੀ ਤੁਸਾਂ ਤੋਂ ਡਰਦਾ ਐ, ਮਤ ਮੋਇਆਂ ਮੇੜ ਮੁਕਾਈਦਾ ।

> ਹੁਣ ਕਿਸ ਥੀਂ ਆਪ ਛੁਪਾਈਦਾ?

"ਮੈਂ" ਮੇਰੀ ਹੈ ਯਾ ਤੇਰੀ ਹੈ? ਇਹ ਅੰਤ ਭਸਮ ਦੀ ਢੇਰੀ ਹੈ,

ਇਹ ਢੇਰੀ ਪੀਆ ਨੇ ਘੇਰੀ ਹੈ, ਢੇਰੀ ਨੂੰ ਨਾਚ ਨਚਾਈਦਾ,

> ਹੁਣ ਕਿਸ ਥੀਂ ਆਪ ਛੁਪਾਈਦਾ?

ਬੁੱਲ੍ਹਾ ਸ਼ੌਹ ਹੁਣ ਸਹੀ ਸਿੰਞਾਤੇ ਹੋ, ਸੂਰਤ ਨਾਲ ਪਛਾਤੇ ਹੋ,

ਕਿਤੇ ਆਤੇ ਹੋ, ਕਿਤੇ ਜਾਤੇ ਹੋ, ਹੁਣ ਮੈਥੋਂ ਭੁੱਲ ਨਾ ਜਾਈਦਾ ।

> ਹੁਣ ਕਿਸ ਥੀਂ ਆਪ ਛੁਪਾਈਦਾ?

کتّے سنت فرض دسیندے او، کتّے ملّاں بانگ بولیندے او ،

کتّے رام دہائی دیندے او، کتّے متھے تلک لگائی دا ،

ہن کس تھیں آپ چھپائیدا ؟

کتّے چور او،کدھرے قاضی او، کتّے منبر تے بہ وعظی او ،

کتّے تیغ بہادر غازی او، آپے پر کٹک چڑھائیدا ،

ہن کس تھیں آپ چھپائیدا ؟

تسی سبھنیں بھیسیں تھیندے او، مدھ آپے آپے پیندے او ،

مینوں ہر جا تسیں دسیندے او ، آپے کو آپ چکائیدا ،

ہن کس تھیں آپ چھپائیدا ؟

جو ڈھونڈ تساڈھی کردا اے ، مویوں اگّے مردا اے ،

مویوں وی تساں تھوں ڈردا اے ، مت مویاں موڑ مکائیدا،

ہن کس تھیں آپ چھپائیدا ؟

"میں" میری ہے یا تیری ہے؟ ایہ انت بھسم دی ڈھیری ہے ،

ایہ ڈھیری پیا نیں گھیری ہے، ڈھیری نوں ناچ نچائیدا،

ہن کس تھیں آپ چھپائیدا ؟

بلھا! شوہ ہن سہی سنجاتے ہو، صورت نال پہچاتے ہو ،

کتّے آتے ہو ، کتّے جاتے ہو، ہن میتھوں بھل نہ جائیدا ،

ہن کس تھیں آپ چھپائیدا ؟

34. They Came to persuade Bulleh (Bulleh noon sumjhawan ayiyan).

They came to persuade Bulleh, his sisters and sisters-in-law.

"Accept o Bullehya, what we say, let go associating with Arrains,

On the line of the Prophet and decendents of Ali, why have you brought shame?"

"Whosoever sees us as a Sayyid, shall be punished in hell,

Whoever calls us an Arrain, shall frolic in paradise!"

Arrains, wandering beggars, all have their place, God does not differentiate,

Like those who shun the prettiest and hold dear the unattractive.

If you are looking for blooming gardens, become a follower of the Arrains,

Why are you asking of Bulleh Shah's caste? Be thankful for his choices.

ਬੁੱਲ੍ਹੇ ਨੂੰ ਸਮਝਾਵਣ ਆਈਆਂ, ਭੈਣਾਂ ਤੇ ਭਰਜਾਈਆਂ।

"ਮੰਨ ਲੈ ਬੁੱਲ੍ਹਿਆ ਸਾਡਾ ਕਹਿਣਾ, ਛੱਡ ਦੇ ਪੱਲਾ ਰਾਈਆਂ"
"ਆਲ ਨਬੀ, ਔਲਾਦ ਅਲੀ ਨੂੰ, ਤੂੰ ਕੀਓ ਲੀਕਾਂ ਲਾਈਆਂ"?

ਜਿਹੜਾ ਸਾਨੂੰ ਸਈਅਦ ਸੱਦੇ, ਦੋਜ਼ਖ ਮਿਲਣ ਸਜ਼ਾਈਆਂ,
ਜੋ ਕੋਈ ਸਾਨੂੰ ਰਾਈਂ ਆਖੇ, ਬਹਿਸ਼ਤੀਂ ਪੀਂਘਾਂ ਪਾਈਆਂ।

ਰਾਈਂ, ਸਾਈਂ ਸਭਨੀ ਥਾਈਂ, ਰੱਬ ਦੀਆਂ ਬੇਪਰਵਾਹੀਆਂ,
ਸੋਹਣੀਆਂ ਪਰ੍ਹੇ ਹਟਾਈਆਂ ਤੇ, ਕੋਝੀਆਂ ਲੈ ਗਲ ਲਾਈਆਂ।

ਜੇ ਤੂੰ ਲੋੜੇਂ ਬਾਗ਼ ਬਹਾਰਾਂ, ਚਾਕਰ ਹੋ ਜਾ ਰਾਈਆਂ,
ਬੁੱਲ੍ਹੇ ਸ਼ਾਹ ਦੀ ਜ਼ਾਤ ਕੀ ਪੁੱਛਨੀ ਏਂ? ਸ਼ਾਕਰ ਹੋ ਰਜ਼ਾਈਆਂ।

بلھے نوں سمجھاون آئیاں بھیناں تے بھرجائیاں ۔

"من لے بلھیا ساڈا کہنا، چھڈ دے پلّا رائیاں"
'' آل نبی، اولاد علی نوں توں کیونہوں لیکاں لائیاں" ؟

جیہڑا سانو سیّد سدّے دوزخ ملن سزا ئیاں ،
جو کوئی سانوں رائیں آکھے، بہشتی پینگھاں پا ئیاں !

رائیں، ساہین سبھنی تھاں، رب دیاں بےپروائیاں ،
سوہنیاں پرے ہٹایاں تے کوجھیاں لے گل لائیاں ۔

جے توں لوڑیں باغ بہاراں، چاکر ہو جا رائیاں ،
بلھے شاہ دی ذات کی پچھنی ایں؟ شاکر ہو رضائیاں ۔

35. Show me your abode (Apna dhus tikaana).

Show me your abode, where did you come from, and where will you go?

The wealth on which you pride yourself,

That will not go with you!

You oppress and torment people,

You have taken the job of feeding off loot.

Wag your tail for these four days,

In the end you will be gone!

You will take your abode in the city of the silent,

Where the world will be confined.

By the armfuls, he takes across, the powerful,

The expert angel of death,

Compared to all the ones here O Bullehya,

He is an ancient professional!

Show me your abode, where did you come from, and where will you go?

ਆਪਣਾ ਦੱਸ ਟਿਕਾਣਾ

ਆਪਣਾ ਦੱਸ ਟਿਕਾਣਾ, ਕਿੱਧਰੋਂ ਆਇਆ, ਕਿੱਧਰ ਜਾਣਾ?

ਜਿਸ ਠਾਣੇ ਦਾ ਮਾਣ ਕਰੇਂ ਤੂੰ,
ਉਹਨੇ ਤੇਰੇ ਨਾਲ ਨਾ ਜਾਣਾ।
ਜ਼ੁਲਮ ਕਰੇਂ ਤੇ ਲੋਕ ਸਤਾਵੇਂ,
ਕਸਬ ਫੜ੍ਹਿਉ ਲੁਟ ਖਾਣਾ।
ਕਰ ਲੈ ਚਾਵੜ ਚਾਰ ਦਿਹਾੜੇ,
ਓੜਕ ਤੂੰ ਉਠ ਜਾਣਾ।
ਸ਼ਹਿਰ-ਖ਼ਮੋਸ਼ਾਂ ਦੇ ਚੱਲ ਵਸ ਸੇ,
ਜਿਥੇ ਮੁਲਕ ਸਮਾਣਾ।
ਭਰ ਭਰ ਪੋਰ ਲੰਘਾਵੇ ਡਾਢਾ,
ਮਲਕ-ਉਲ-ਮੌਤ ਮਹਾਣਾ।
ਇਨ੍ਹਾਂ ਸਭਨਾਂ ਥੀਂ ਏ, ਬੁੱਲ੍ਹਿਆ,
ਐਗੁਣਹਾਰ ਪੁਰਾਣਾ।

ਆਪਣਾ ਦੱਸ ਟਿਕਾਣਾ, ਕਿੱਧਰੋਂ ਆਇਆ, ਕਿੱਧਰ ਜਾਣਾ?

اپنا دس ٹکانا، کدھروں آیا ، کدھر جانا ؟

جس ٹھانے دا مان کریں توں ،

اوہنے ترے نال نہ جانا ۔

ظلم کریں تے لوک ستاویں،

کسب پھڑیو لٹ کھانا ۔

کر لے چاوڑ چار دیہاڑے ،

اوڑک توں اٹھ جانا ۔

شہر خموشاں دے چل وسسے ،

جتھے ملک سمانا ۔

بھر بھر پور لنگھاوے ڈاہڈا ،

ملک الموت مہانا ۔

ایہناں سبھناں تھیں اے بلھیا ،

او گنہار پرانا ۔

اپنا دس ٹکانہ، کدھروں آیا ، کدھر جانا ؟

36.   True love (Ishq).

I entered the Ministry of True Love,

Thereafter, True Love took away my reasoning,

I had gone to get acclaim from True Love,

Thereafter, True Love took away my admittance.

True Love robs Messengers and Prophets,

It has stolen many kingdoms from their kings,

What has been stolen from you yet Bullehya?

This True Love has stolen God's whole creation!

ਇਸ਼ਕ

ਐਨ ਇਸ਼ਕ ਦੇ ਮਹਿਕਮੇ ਮੈਂ ਵੜਿਆ,

ਅੱਗੋਂ ਇਸ਼ਕ ਨੇ ਮੇਰੀ ਦਾਨਾਈ ਲੁੱਟ ਲਈ,

ਮੈਂ ਗਿਆ ਸਾਂ ਇਸ਼ਕ ਕੋਲੋਂ ਦਾਦ ਲੈਵਣ,

ਅੱਗੋਂ ਇਸ ਨੇ ਮੇਰੀ ਰਸਾਈ ਲੁੱਟ ਲਈ।

ਇਸ਼ਕ ਲੁੱਟਦਾ ਏ ਨਬੀ ਪੈਗੰਬਰਾਂ ਨੂੰ,

ਕਈ ਬਾਦਸ਼ਾਹਾਂ ਦੀ ਬਾਦਸ਼ਾਹੀ ਲੁੱਟ ਲਈ,

ਅਜੇ ਤੇਰਾ ਕੀ ਲੁੱਟਿਆ ਏ ਬੁੱਲ੍ਹਿਆ,

ਐਸ ਇਸ਼ਕ ਨੇ ਖੁਦਾ ਦੀ ਖੁਦਾਈ ਲੁੱਟ ਲਈ।

۳٦.   عشق

عین عشق دے محکمے میں وڑیا،
اگوں عشق نیں میری دانائی لٹ لیئی ،
میں گیا ساں عشق کولوں داد لیون،
اگوں عشق نیں میری رسائی لٹ لیئی ۔

عشق لٹدا اے نبی پیغمبران نوں ،
کئی بادشاہاں دی بادشاہی لٹ لیئی ،
اجیں تیرا کی لٹیا اے بلھیا ،
ایس عشق نیں خدا دی خدائی لٹ لیئی

37.   Ego (Nafs).

Chanting God, God, have become old, mullahs and pandits all,

They found no hint of God, becoming weary of their prostrations!

But God resides within you, in the Quran are signs,

Bulleh Shah, God will be found by him, who kills his own ego!

ਨਫਸ

ਰੱਬ ਰੱਬ ਕਰਦੇ ਬੁੱਢੇ ਹੋ ਗਏ, ਮੁੱਲਾਂ ਪੰਡਤ ਸਾਰੇ,
ਰੱਬ ਦਾ ਖੋਜ ਖੁਰਾ ਨਾ ਲੱਭਾ, ਸਜਦੇ ਕਰ ਕਰ ਹਾਰੇ।

ਰਬ ਤੇ ਤੇਰੇ ਅੰਦਰ ਵੱਸਦਾ, ਵਿੱਚ ਕੁਰਾਨ ਇਸ਼ਾਰੇ,
ਬੁੱਲੇ ਸ਼ਾਹ, ਰਬ ਉਹਨੂੰ ਮਿਲਸੀ, ਜਿਹੜਾ ਅਪਨੇ ਨਫਸ ਨੂੰ
ਮਾਰੇ।

٣٧.   نفس

رب رب کردے بڈھے ہو گئے، ملاں پنڈ ت سارے،
رب دا کھوج کھرا نہ لبھا ، سجدے کر کر ہارے -

رب تے تیرے اندر وسدا، وچ قرآن اشارے ،
بلھے شاہ ، رب اوہنو ملسی، جیڑا اپنے نفس نوں مارے -

38.   Friend (Yaar).

The friend who has a thousand friends,

Don't consider that friend a friend,

He who loves you beyond limits,

Don't consider that love as love.

He be a friend and cause you a loss,

Don't consider that loss a loss,

Bulleh Shah, no matter how poor your friend may be,

Don't consider his fellowship as worthless!

ਯਾਰ।

ਜਿਸ ਯਾਰ ਦੇ ਯਾਰ ਹਜ਼ਾਰ ਹੋਵਣ,
ਉਸ ਯਾਰ ਨੂੰ ਯਾਰ ਨਾ ਸਮਝੀਂ,
ਜਿਹੜਾ ਹੱਦ ਤੋਂ ਵੱਧਕੇ ਪਿਆਰ ਕਰੇ,
ਉਸ ਪਿਆਰ ਨੂੰ ਪਿਆਰ ਨਾ ਸਮਝੀਂ।

ਹੋਵੇ ਯਾਰ ਤੇ ਦੇਵੇ ਹਾਰ,
ਉਸ ਹਾਰ ਨੂੰ ਹਾਰ ਨਾ ਸਮਝੀਂ,
ਬੁੱਲੇ ਸ਼ਾਹ, ਭਾਵੇਂ ਯਾਰ ਜਿੰਨਾ ਵੀ ਗ਼ਰੀਬ ਹੋਵੇ,
ਉਹਦੀ ਸੰਗਤ ਨੂੰ ਬੇਕਾਰ ਨਾ ਸਮਝੀਂ।

٣٨.   یار ۔

جس یار دے یار ہزار ہوون ،
اس یار نوں یار نہ سمجیں ،
جیڑا حد توں ود کے پیار کرے ،
اس پیار نوں پیار نہ سمجیں ۔

ہووے یار تے دیوے ہار ،
اس ہار نوں ہار نہ سمجھیں ،
بلھے شاہ ، پھویں یارجنا وی غریب ہووے ،
اودی سنگت نوں بیکار نہ سمجھیں ۔

39. This true Love (Ais Ishq).

This True love has a strange tradition,

It robs you in the meeting of an eye,

Others rob by becoming your enemies,

But this robs you by making you a friend!

Where True love has barely glimpsed,

There, wisdom has lost all reasoning,

Getting them to grasp begging bowls,

This true love robs sons of Kings!

ਐਸ ਇਸ਼ਕ

ਐਸ ਇਸ਼ਕ ਦੀ ਰੀਤ ਅਨੋਖੀ ਏ,
ਐਹ ਤੇ ਨੈਣ ਮਿਲਾ ਕੇ ਲੁੱਟ ਲੈਂਦਾ,
ਲੋਕੀ ਦੁਸ਼ਮਣ ਬਨਾ ਕੇ ਲੁੱਟਦੇ ਨੇ,
ਇਹ ਤੇ ਯਾਰ ਬਣਾ ਕੇ ਲੁੱਟ ਲੈਂਦਾ।

ਜਿੱਥੇ ਇਸ਼ਕ ਨੇ ਝਾਤੀ ਪਾਈ ਐ,
ਉੱਥੇ ਅਕਲ ਨੇ ਹੋਸ਼ ਗਵਾਈ ਐ,
ਐਹ ਬਾਦਸ਼ਾਹਾਂ ਦੇ ਪੁੱਤਰਾਂ ਨੂੰ,
ਹੱਥ ਕਾਸੇ ਫੜਾ ਕੇ ਲੁੱਟ ਲੈਂਦਾ।

٣٩.   ایس عشق

ایس عشق دی ریت انوکھی اے ،
ایہ تے نین ملا کے لٹ لیندا ،
لوکی دشمن بنا کے لٹدے نے،
ایہ تے یار بنا کے لٹ لیندا ۔

جتھے عشق نیں جھاتی پایی اے ،
اوتھے عقل نیں ہوش گوایی اے ،
ایہ بادشاہاں دے پتراں نوں ،
ہتھ کاسے پھڑا کے لٹ لیندا ۔

111

40. Ram, Raheem and Maula (Ram, Raheem tai Maula).

If you have truely understood, then what's the commotion?

What then is this Ram, Raheem and Maula?

ਰਾਮ ਰਹੀਮ ਤੇ ਮੌਲਾ ।

ਗੱਲ ਸਮਝ ਲਈ ਏ ਤਾਂ ਰੌਲਾ ਕੀ?
ਇਹ ਰਾਮ ਰਹੀਮ ਤੇ ਮੌਲਾ ਕੀ?

٤٠.   رام ، رحیم تے مولا -

گل سمج لیہی اے تے فر رولا کی ؟
ایہ رام ، رحیم تے مولا کی ؟

The shrine and last resting place of Baba Bulleh Shah, Kasur, Punjab, Pakistan

Image credit: tribune.com.pk (2010)

Part 2 – Transliteration.

1. Jai Rab Milda.

Jai Rab milda nahateyan dhoteyan,

Tai O milda dudduan mucchiyan noon!

Jai Rab milda jungle baillayan,

Tai O milda ganhiyan bucchiyan noon!

Jai Rab milda mandir maseeti,

Tai O milda cham chirrikiyaan noon!

Ve Bullehya, Rab ohnan noon milda,

Jinnan diyan neetan howun succhiyan!

2. Muqeed.

Jai main tainu undher dhoondhan,

Tai phair muqeed main jannan,

Jai main tainu bhahur dhoondhan,

Tai meray undher kon summana?

Sub kuj toon ain, sub wich toon ain,

Sub toon Pak pechanhan,

Main vee toon ain, toon vee main han,

Wut Bullah kon nimana?

3. Ishq sammundar.

Luq, luq jeena, tai murna ki?

Inj hona ki, tai kurna ki?

Judoon ishq sammundray kudh jannaran,

Phair dubna ki, tai turna ki?

4. Naazuk dil.

Ussi naazuk dil dai bundhay han,

Saddha dil nah yaar dukkhaya kar,

Nah jhoothay waadhay kurya kar,

Nah jhoothian kusman chaaya kar!

Tainu kinni waari main akkhya ai,

Mainu vul vul nah uzmaaya kar!

Teri yaad dai wich main mur jassan,

Mainu itna yaad nah ayya kar!

5.   Churrdhay suraj.

Churrdhay suraj dhuldhay waikhay,

Bujjay diway buldhay waikhay,

Heeray da koi mool nah taaray,

Khottay sikkay chuldhay waikhay!

Jinnan da nah ai jug tai koi,

Oh vee puttar puldhay waikhay,

Ohdhee rehmat dai naal o bundhya,

Bundhay panni uttay chuldhay waikhay!

Loki kehndhay daal nehin guldi,

Ussan putthur guldhay waikhay!

Jinnan kuder nah kitti Yaar dee Bullehya,

Huth khali o muldhay waikhay!

6. Firka-bundhi.

Ik passay rehn Wahhabi, ik passay Deobandi,

Uggay picchay Shia, Sunni, dhaadhi firka-bundhi.

Wich wuchalay saadha kotha, kismat saadhi mundhi,

Ik mohalla, utth maseetan, kehdhi kurran pabundhi!

7. Ik nuktay wich.

Phurrh nukta, chorrh hussaban noon,

Chuddh dozakh, gorr azzaban noon,

Kar bundh kufr daiyaan baaban noon,

Kar saaf dillay daiyan khaaban noon,

Gul aissay ghur wich dhookdhi ai!

Ik nuktay wich gul mukdhi ai!

Ehwain muttha, zameen ghusaai dha,

Paa lumma mehraab, dukhaai dha,

Purrh Kalima lok hussaai dha,

Dil undher summuj nah- lai dha,

Kudhi succhi gul vee lukdhi ai?

Ik nuktay wich gul mukdhi ai!

Ik Jungle, behreen jandhay neen,

Ik danna roz dha khandhay neen,

Bay- summuj wajood thukkanday neen,

Ghar aawan ho k mandhay neen,

Ehwain chillayyan wich jindh sukdhi ai!

Ik nuktay wich gul mukdhi ai!

Phurrh Murshid, abd Khuddahi ho,

Wich musti, bay-purwahi ho,

Bay-khaahish, bay-nuwwai ho,

Wich dil dai khoob succhayi ho,

Bullehya, kudhi succhi gul vee rukdhi ai?

Ik nuktay wich gul mukdhi ai!

8. Ghur bettha.

Purrh, purrh alim faazul hoya-ain,

Kudhi uprrain aap noon purrhiya he nehin!

Ja, ja wurrdha ain mandir, maseetan,

Kudhi mun uprrain wich wurrhiya he nehin!

Ehwain rose shaitan nal lurrdha ain,

Kudhi nufs uprrain nal lurriya he nehin!

Bulleh Shah! usmaani ud-dhiyan phurrna ain,

Jehrra ghur bettha ohnoo phurriya he nehin!

9.   Bullehya! ki jannan main kon.

Nah main Momin, wich maseetan,

Nah main wich kufr diyan reetan,

Nah main paakan wich paleetan,

Nah main Mussa, nah Firrown!

                              Bullehya! Ki jannan main kon.

Nah main wich paleeti paaki,

Nah wich shaadi , nah ghumnaki,

Nah main aabi, nah main khaki,

Nah main attish, nah wich paun!

                              Bullehya! Ki jannan main kon.

Nah main undher Vedh kitaaban,

Nah wich bhunghan, nah shraaban,

Nah wich rindan must khraaban,

Nah wich jaggun, nah wich saun,

                              Bullehya! Ki jannan main kon.

Nah main bhaidh muzhab dha paaya,

Nah main Adam, Huwa jaaya,

Nah kuj apna naam dhurraya,

Nah wich baithen, nah wich bhoan,

                              Bullehya! Ki jannan main kon.

Awul akhir aap noon jannan,

Nah koi dooja hor pichanan,

Mehthoon horun nah koi siyanna,

Bullehya! ahho khurra hai kon?

                              Bullehya! Ki jannan main kon.

10.   Kuttay tehthoon uttay!

Raatin jaggain, shaikh sudhawain,

Raatin jaggun kuttay, tehthoon uttay!

Bhonkan toon bundh mool nah hondhay,

Ja rorrih tai suttay, tehthoon uttay!

Khussam apnay dha dhur nah chuddhay,

Phanwain wujjan juttay, tehthoon uttay!

Bulleh Shah! koi rikht wehaj lai,

Nehin tai baazi lai gai kuttay, tehthoon uttay!

11. Undher, baaher.

Ghussay wich nah ayya kar,

Thunda kar kay khaaya kar,

Din teray vee phir jaan gai,

Ehwain nah ghubraaya kar!

Pyaar dai aissay bootay laa,

Sarray pind tai saaya kar,

Upnay undroon jhooth mukaa,

Such dha dhol wujaaya kar!

Rukkhi sukkhi kha kay toon,

Sujday wich tur jaaya kar,

Mun undher toon jharoo dai,

Undher baaher suffaaya kar!

12.   Hindu nah, naahin Mussalman.

Hindu nah, naahin Mussalman,
Behay trinjin, tej abhimaan.

Sunni nah, naahin hum shia,
Sullah Kull ka marg liyya.

Phukkhay nah, naahin hum rujjay,
Nunggay nah, naahin hum kujjay.

Rondhay nah, naahin hum husdhay,
Ujrray nah, naahin hum wusdhay.

Paapi nah, sudhermi nah,
Paap pun ki rah nah jaan.

Bulleh Shah! Jo hur chit laggay,
Hindu, Turk dojan tiyagay!

13. Mukkay gaiyan.

Mukkay gaiyan gull mukdhi naahin,

Pahwain sau sau jummay purrh ayiyay.

Ganga gaiyan gull mukdhi naahin,

Pahwain sau sau ghottay khaaiyay.

Gaya gaiyan gull mukdhi naahin,

Pahwain sau sau pundh purrhaiyay.

Bulleh Shah gul taanhiyoon mukdhi,

Judoon "mai" noon dilloon guwwaiyay!

14.   Tuhiyoon ain!

Tuhiyoon ain, main naa hin, sujna,
Tuhiyoon ain, main naa hin!

Khollay dai purchawain wangoon, ghoom reha mun naa hin,
Jai bollan tunh nallay bollain, chuup ruhwan mun naa hin,
Jai sonhwan tunh nallay sonhwain, jai turrhan tunh raahin,
Bullehya! Shao ghur ayya meray, jindri gholl ghumayhin!

Tuhiyoon ain, main naa hin sujna,
Tuhiyoon ain, main naa hin!

15. Mandir dha dai.

Mandir dha dai, masjid dha dai,

Dha dai jo kuj dhaindha,

Ik, bundhay dha dil nah dhaween,

Kay Rab dillan wich rhendha!

16.   Ilmoon bus kurrin o yaar!

Ilmoon bus kurrin o yaar,
Ikko Alif terray durkar!

Ilim nah awway wich shummar,
Jandhi ummar, nehin aitbar,
Ikko Alif terray durkar,
Ilmoon bus kurrin o yaar!

Ilmoon bus kurrin o yaar!

Purrh, purrh, likh, likh, lawain dhair,
Dhair kitaaban char chophair,
Girdhay channan, wich unhair,
Puccho "Rah" tai khubbur nah saar,

Ilmoon bus kurrin o yaar!

Purrh, purrh nuffal, namaz ghuzzarain,
Ucchiyan baangan chaangan marrain,
Mimbar tai churrh whaaz pukkarain,
Keeta tainu ilim khwaar!

Ilmoon bus kurrin o yaar!

Ilmoon pai kizziyai hor,
Akhaan wallay unnhay korr,
Phurrdhay saadh tai chuddhun chor,
Dohin jehannin hon khwaar!

Ilmoon bus kurrin o yaar!

Purrh, purrh, Shaikh mushaaikh kuhawain,

Ultay musslay ghurroon bunnawain,

Bay-Ilmaan noon lut lut khawain,

Jhoothay, succhay kurrain iqrar!

                              Ilmoon bus kurrin o yaar!

Purrh, purrh mullan hoy Qazi,

Allah ilmaan bahjoon razi,

Howay hirs dinno din tazi,

Tainu kita hirs khwaar!

                              Ilmoon bus kurrin o yaar!

Purrh, Purrh musslay peya sunawain,

Khanna shuk, shubbay dha khawain,

Dhussain hor tai hor kummawain,

Undher khot, baher suchyaar!

                              Ilmoon bus kurrin o yaar!

Judh main sabq ishq dha purrhaiya,

Durriya waikh wahiddut dha wurrhaiya,

Ghummun gheeran dai wich urrhaiya,

Shah Innayat laaya par!

                              Ilmoon bus kurrin o

yaar!

17. Koi Puccho!

Koi puccho dilbar ki kurdha?

          Eh jo kurdha so kurdha!

Wich maseet namaz guzzaray,

          Buut-khannay ja wurrdha!

Aap iko, kai lakh ghurran dai,

          Malik hai ghur ghur dha!

Iksay ghur wich rusdhay wusdhay nahin,

          Rehndha wich purdah!

Jit wul waikkhan, utt wul ohhoo,

          Hur dhi sunggat kurdha!

Wahidat dai durriya dai undher,

          Sub jug dissay turdha!

Bullehya! Shaoo dha ishq bagheela,

          Rutti painda, ghosht churrdha!

Koi puccho dilbar ki kurdha?

          Eh jo kurdha so kurdha!

18. Kaissi toba?

Kaissi toba hai eh toba? Aissi toba nah kar yaar!

Munhoon toba, dilloon nah kurdha,

Iss toba theen turk nah phurdha,

Kiss ghuflat nain paayau purdah,

Tainu bukhshay kyuoon Ghuffaar?

Sanu dai kay loyeen suwaayai,

Dhadhayan uttay baazi laayai,

Mussallmani oh kidhroon paayai,

Jis dha howay eh kirdar?

Jit nah jaana, othay jawain,

Huq beganna mukr khawain,

Korr kitaaban sir tai chawwain,

Howay ki tera aitbaar?

Zaalim zulmoon naahin durdhay,

Apni kittiyoon appay murdhay,

Nah hin khauf Khuda dha kurdhay,

Aithay, othay howwan khwaar!

Kaissi toba hai eh toba? Aissi toba nah kar yaar!

19. Kamil Murshid.

Bulleh noon lok muttinh daindhay,

                    toon jah bhao maseeti!

Wich maseetan ki kuj hondha,

                    jai dilloon namaz nah neeti?

Bharoon paak keetay ki hondha,

                    jai undroon nah gaiyi paleeti?

Bin kamil murshid Bullehya,

                    teri ehwain gaiyi ibbadat keeti!

20. Ik Alif purrho!

Ik Alif purrho chutkara ai.

Ik alfoon, dou, tin, chaar hoyai,

Phir lakh, carore, huzzaar hoyai,

Phir othoon bajh shumaar hoyai,

Ais Alif dha nukta niyaara ai,

                    Ik Alif purrho chutkara ai.

Kyuoon hoya ain shukul jilladan dhi,

Kyuoon purrhna ain gudh kitaaban dhi,

Sir chaana ain pundh azaaban dhi,

Uggay painda mushkil pharrah ai,

                    Ik Alif purrho chutkara ai.

Bin Hafiz hifz Quran Karrain,

Purrh Purrh kay saaf zubaan karrain,

Pur nehmat wich dheyaan karrain,

Mun phirdha jeevain hulkara ai,

                    Ik Alif purrho chutkara ai.

21. Bus kar ji.

Bus kar ji, hunh bus kar ji,
Ik baat ussan naal huss kar ji.

Seenh dil meray wich wusdhay o,
Ehwain sathyoon dhoor kyuoon nusdhay o,
Nallay ghut jaddoo dil khusdhay o,

          Bus kar ji, hunh bus kar ji.

Seenh moyyan noon maar mukaindhay si,
Nit Kaidho waang kuttaindhay si,
Gul kurdaiyan dha gulla ghutaindhay si,
Hun teer luggao kuss kar ji,

          Bus kar ji, hunh bus kar ji.

Seenh chupdhay o, ussan pukkray o,
Ussan naal zulf dai jukkray o,
Seenh ajain chuppan toon tukkray o,
Hunh jaan nah milda nuss kar ji,

          Bus kar ji, hunh bus kar ji.

Bulleh, Shaoo main teri burdhi aan,
Tera mukkh waikhun noon murdhi aan,
Nit sau sau mintan kurdhi aan,
Hun baith pinjer wich dhuss kar ji,

          Bus kar ji, hunh bus kar ji.

22.   Rab tai bundhay di zaat.

Rab tai bundhay di zaat ikko,

Jeevain kuppray di zaat ai roonh,

Rab bundhay wich inj lukkiya,

Jeevain kuppray wich lukkiya ai roonh!

Aap bullaway, tai appay he bollay,

Appay he kurdha ai "Hoon",

Kamil murshid mil jaayai Bullehya,

Tai nah "main" rehiyay, tai nah "toon".

23. Gori ya kaali.

Kissay keeta suwaal Mian Majnu noon,

Teri Laila tai rung dhi kaali ai,

Ditta juwab Mian Majnu nai,

Teri akkh nah waikhan walli ai.

Quran paak dai warq nai chittay,

Uttay likhee sehaahi kaali ai,

Chuud way Bullehya, dil dai chuddeya,

Tai phir ki gori tai ki kaali ai!

24.   Utth jaag!

Utth jaag! ghurrareh maar nehin, ai saun terray durkaar nehin!

Kitthay hai Sultan Sukkundar? Maut nah chuddhay Pir Paighumber,

Subhay chud chud gai addumber, koi aithay paaidhar nehin!

Jo kuj kursain, so kuj passain, nehin tai aurruck puchtasain,

Soonjhi koonj wangoon kurllasain, khummban bahj uddaar nehin!

Bulleh! Shaoo bin koi nah hin, aithay othay dowain serrayin,

Sumbhal sumbhal kuddham tikayeen, phair awwun dooji waar nehin!

Utth jaag, ghurrareh maar nehin, ai saun terray durkaar nehin!

25. Ghurryali daiwo nikaal ni!

Ghurryali daiwo nikaal ni,

Mera pia ghur ayya, laal ni.

Ghurri ghurri ghurryal bujaway,

Rain wissul dhi pia ghuttaway,

Meray mun dhi baat jai paaway,

Huthoon cha soottay ghurryal ni!

Ghurryali daiwo nikaal ni!

Un-hudh baja bujjay suhannah,

Muttrib! sukkhra taan traanah,

Bhulla saum, Sallat dou-gaanah,

Mudh piyalla dain kullal ni!

Ghurryali daiwo nikaal ni

Dukh dillidar utth gia saara,

Mukh waikhya tai ajub nazzara,

Rain wuddhi, kuj kurro pussara,

Din uggay dhurro diwaal ni!

Ghurryali daiwo nikaal ni.

Bullehya! Shaoo dhi saij piyaari,

Ni main taar nihaaray taari,

Kuvin kuvin meri ayyi waari,

Hunh wichraan hoya muhaal ni!

Ghurryali daiwo nikaal ni.

Mera pia ghur ayya, lhal ni.

26. Okha!

Jhulleya..., ishq kummana okha!

Kissay noon yaar bunnana okha!

Pyar pyar tai har koi kookay,

Kar kay pyaar, nibhana okha!

Har koi dukhaan tai huns lainda,

Kissay dha durdh wundowna okha!

Gullan nal nai Sufi rutbay milday,

Jogi bhes wuttana okha!

Koi kissay dhi gull nehin sunhdha,

Lokaan noon sumjhana okha!

27. Punchi.

Vaikh bundhia usmanan uddhay punchi,
Vaikh tay sehi ki kurdhay nay.
Nah oh kurdhay rizq zakheera,
Nah oh phukkhay murdhay nay!

Kudhi kissay nay pankh pakkhera,
Phukkhay murdhay waikhay nay?
Bundhay he kurdhay nain rizq zahkheera,
Bundhay he phukkhay murdhay nay!

28.   Tawheed.

Ilim purrhyan ashraaf nah howan,

Jehrrhay howan ussul kaminay,

Pittal kudhi nahin sona bun-dha,

Phaawain jurrhiyay laal nagginay!

Shoom thin kudhi nehin sadqa hondha,

Phaawain howan lakh khazinay,

Bullehya! bhaj tawheed nehin jannat milni,

Phawain murriyay wich Madinnay!

29. Main bay-kaidh!

Main bay-kaidh anh, main bay-kaidh,

                Nah rogi nah vaidh.

Nah main momin, nah main kafir,

                Nah sayyid nah saidh.

Chaudhwin tabkinh sirrah saddah,

                Kittay nah howiyay kaidh.

Khrabbat main jaal assadi,

                Nah showbha nah aib.

Bulleh Shah di zaat ki puchni ain?

                Nah paidah nah- paidh.

Main bay-kaidh anh, main bay-kaidh.

30.   Ranjha, Ranjha.

Ranjha, Ranjha kurdhi hun main, appay Ranjha hoi,
Suddu mainu deedo Ranjha, Heer nah akkho koi.

Ranjha mai vich, mai Ranjhay vich, ghair khyaal nah koi,
Mai nehin, ohoo aap hai, apni aap kurray diljoi.

Jo kuj saadhay undher dhissay, zaat assadhi sohi,
Jis dai naal main newnh luggaya, ohoo jaissi hoi.

Chitti chaddhur lah sut kurriyay, pehen fakiraan loi,
Chitti chaddhur daagh luggaisi, loi daagh nah koi.

Takht Hazzaray lai chul Bullehya, Siyaalin millay nah dhoi,
Ranjha, Ranjha kurdhi hun main appay Ranjha hoi.

31.   Haji lok.

Haji lok Makkay wal jandhay,

Mera Ranjha mahi Makkah,

Ni main kamli anh!

Main mung Ranjhay yaar di hoiyaan,

Mera babul kardha dhukka,

Ni main kamli anh!

Haji lok Makkay wal jandhay,

Meray ghur wich nau sau Makkah,

Ni main kamli anh!

Wicchay Haji, wicchay Qazi,

Wicchay chor acchucka,

Ni main kamli anh!

Haji lok Makkay wal jandhay,

Assi janna Takht Hazzaray,

Ni main kamli anh!

Jit wal yaar, uttay wal Kaaba,

Phaawain phol kitabaan charray!

Ni main kamli anh!

32. Ultay hor zummanay ayai.

Ultay hor zumanay ayai,
Tanh main bhaid sujjan dai paayai.

Kaanh luggran noo marrun luggay, chirriyan jurray dhayai
Ghorray chugghan urrorhian tai ghuddhoon khweed puwayai.

Upniyan wich ulfat nah hin, ki chaachay ki taayai,
Piu puttran itfaq nah kaahi, dhiyaan naal nah maayai.

Succhyan noon pay milday dhukkay, jhoothay kol bahayai,
Uglay ho kunghalay baithay, pichlayan fursh wicchayai.

Bhorriyan wallay Rajjay kittay, Rajjayan bheek munghayai,
Bullehya! hukm Hazooroon ayya, tiss noon kon huttayai.

Ultay hor zumanay ayai,
Tanh main bhaid sujjan dai paayai.

33. Hunh kis thin aap chuppai dha?

Kittay sunnat, farz dusaindhay ho, kittay mullan baang bolaindhay ho,

Kittay Ram dohaee daindhay ho, kittay mutthay tilak laggai dha,

> Hunh kis thin aap
chuppai dha?

Kittay chorr ho kidhray Qazi ho, kittay mimbar tai beh wahzi ho,

Kittay Tegh Bahadur Ghazi ho, aapay par katak churrhai dha,

> Hunh kis thin aap
chuppai dha?

Tussin subhain bhessin thaindhay ho, mudh aapay appay peendhay ho,

Mainu har ja tussin dusaindhay ho, appay ko aap chukkai dha,

> Hunh kis thin aap
chuppai dha?

Jo dhoondh tussadhi kurdha ai, moyaan tunh uggay murdha ai,

Moyaan vee tussan thoon durdha ai, mutt moyaan morr mukkahi dha,

> Hunh kis thin aap
chuppai dha?

"Main" meri hai ya teri hai? Eh ant bhussam dhi dhairi hai,

Eh dhairi pia nain ghairi hai, dhairi noon naach nucchaee dha,

> Hunh kis thin aap
chuppai dha?

Bullah, Shaoo hunh sehi sunjatay ho, soorat nal pehchatay ho,

Kittay attay ho, kittay jattay ho, hunh maithoon bhul nah jai dha,

> Hunh kis thin aap
chuppai dha?

34. Bulleh noon sumjhawan ayiyan.

Bulleh noon sumjhawan ayiyan bhenan tai bhurjahiyan.

"Mun lai Bullehya, saddah kehna, chudd dai pulla raaiyan,

Aal Nabi, aulad Ali noon, toonh kyuhoon leekan laaiyan?"

"Jehra sannu Sayyid sudday dozakh millen suzzaiyan,

Jo koi sanu Arrain akkhay, beheshti peenghan paaiyan!"

Arrain, Saayin subnhi thanh ein, Rab diyan bay- purwahiyan,

Sohniyan purray huttaiyan tai koojian lai gul laaiyan.

Jai toonh lorrain bagh beharran, chaaker ho ja raaiyan,

Bulleh Shah di zaat ki puchni-en? Shaaker ho ruzzaiyan.

35. Apna dhus tikaana.

Apna dhus tikaana, kidhroon ayya, kidher jaana?

Jis thaanay dha maan kurrain toonh,

Ohnay terray naal nah jaana!

Zulm kurrain tai lok suttawain,

Kussab phurryo lut khaana!

Kur lai chaawurrh char dehaaray,

Aurak toonh utth jaana!

Sher khamoshan dai chul vussesay,

Jithay mulk sumanha!

Bhur bhur paure lunghaway dhaadha,

Mulk-ul-mott mohana,

Ehnan sabnanh thinh hai Bullehya,

Oh gunnhaar puranha.

Apna dhus tikaana, kidhroon ayya, kidher jaana?

36. Ishq.

Ain ishq dai mehkammay main vurrhya,

Aghun ishq nain meri daanai lut lai,

Main gia saan ishq kolloon daadh lewan,

Aghun ishq nain meri russai lut lai.

Ishq lutdha ai Nabi Peghamberan noon,

Kaee badshahan dhi badshai lut lai,

Ajain tera ki luteya aye o Bullehya?

Ais isqh nain khuda dhi khuddai lut lai!

37. Nafs.

Rab Rab kurdhay buddhay ho gai, mullan, pandit sarray,

Rab dha khoj khurrah nah lubha, sujday kar kar harray!

Rab tay tairray undher wusdah, wich Quran issharay,

Bullay Shah, Rab ohnoo milsi, jehra apnay nafs noon marray!

38.   Yaar.

Jis yaar dai yaar huzaar howan,

Uss yaar noon yaar nah samjheen,

Jehra hudh toon wudh kay pyaar kurray,

Uss pyaar noon pyaar nah samjheen.

Howay yaar tay daiway haar,

Uss haar noon haar nah samjheen,

Bulleh Shah, phawain yaar jinna vee ghareeb howay,

Ohdhee sangat noon baykar nah samjheen!

39.   Ais Ishq.

Ais ishq dhi reet anokhi ai,

Eh tay nain mila kay lut lainda,

Loki dushman bunna kay lut dai nai,

Eh tay yaar bunna kay lut lainda.

Jitthay ishq nain jhaati paayi ai,

Othay akul nain hosh gwaee ai,

Eh badshahan dai puttran noon,

Huth kassay phurra kay lut lainda!

40. Ram, Raheem tai Maula.

Gal sammuj lai ai tai phir raula ki?

Eh Ram, Raheem tai Maula ki?

Printed in Great Britain
by Amazon

41180186R00107